Programs
for
Lent
and
Easter

Volume 2

PROGRAMS FOR LENT AND EASTER, VOLUME 2

Copyright © 1983
Judson Press, Valley Forge, PA 19482-0851

The name JUDSON PRESS is registered as a trademark in the U.S. Patent Office. Printed in the U.S.A. ⊕

The programs, plays, pageants, and ideas in this book were originally published in the February, 1980; March, 1980; February, 1981; March, 1981; March, 1982; February, 1983; and March, 1983 issues of *Baptist Leader*. All of the programs were used successfully by churches across the country.

Art and Photograph Credits: pp. 6, 33, Unada Gliewe; pp. 9-11, 21-22, 30-32, Bill Hamilton; pp. 19, 23, Paul M. Schrock; pp. 25, 27, 42, 44, Three Lions; p. 29, American Museum of Photography; p. 34, Wallowitch; p. 35, David Hiebert; p. 39, Vernon Sigl; p. 41, Marie Layne; pp. 50, 51, Vonnie Farra; pp. 49, 56, 63, Camerique.

Programs *for* Lent *and* Easter

Volume 2

Compiled and edited by Vincie Alessi

Judson Press® Valley Forge

Triumph

O Christ—

   I'm so glad you came to live

   Upon this earth as other mortals do—

   So glad you felt the sun

     And heard the wind

     As it whistled through the trees.

   I'm so glad you chose

   To be as other humans are—

     To laugh and love and lift.

   And last of all,

   I'm glad you died—

     And rose triumphant

      From the grave

   To save me

     From all this world's sin.

—Nina Jean Meth
Newport News, Virginia

Contents

Philip

● by Harry Pritchett, Jr.

"For you who don't believe in miracles, I want
to tell you that one happened on that day last
spring. Thank God, miracles can and do
happen."

Once upon a time I had a young friend named Philip. Philip lived in a nearby city, and Philip was born with Down's syndrome. He was a pleasant child—happy, it seemed—but increasingly aware of the difference between himself and other children. Philip went to Sunday school. His teacher also was a friend of mine. My teacher friend taught the third grade at the Methodist church. Philip was in the class with nine other eight-year-old boys and girls.

Most of you know eight-year-olds. And Philip, with his differences, was not readily accepted as a member of his third-grade Sunday school class. But my friend was a creative teacher, and he helped to facilitate a good group of eight-year-old children. They learned, and they laughed, and they played together. And they really cared about one another, even though, as you know, eight-year-olds don't often say out loud that they care about one another. But my teacher friend could see it. He knew it. He also knew that Philip was not really a part of that group of children. *Philip, of course, did not choose nor did he want to be different. He just was. And that was just the way things were.*

My Sunday school teacher friend had a marvelous design for his class on the Sunday after Easter last year. You know those things that pantyhose come in—the containers that look like great big eggs—my friend had collected thirty of these to use on that Sunday. The children loved it when he brought them into the room. Each child was to get a great big egg. It was a beautiful spring day, and the assigned task was for each child to go outside on the church grounds and to find a symbol for new life, put it into the egg, and bring it back to the classroom. They would then open and share their new life symbols and surprises together one by one.

Well, they did this, and it was glorious. And it was confusing. And it was wild. They ran all around, gathered their symbols, and returned to the classroom. They put all the big eggs on a table, and then the teacher opened them.

He opened one. There was a flower, and they ooed and aahed. He opened another, and there was a little butterfly. "Beautiful," the girls all said, since it is hard for eight-year-old boys to say "beautiful." He opened another, and there was a rock. And as third graders will, some laughed, and some said, "That's crazy! How's a rock supposed to be like new life?" But the smart little boy whose egg they were speaking of spoke up. He said, "That's mine. And I knew all of you would get flowers, and buds, and leaves, and butterflies, and stuff like that. So I got a rock because I wanted to be different. And for me, that's new life." They all laughed. My teacher friend said something to himself about the profundity of eight-year-olds and went on opening egg surprises.

He opened the next one, and there was nothing there. The other children, as eight-year-olds will, said, "That's not fair! That's stupid! Somebody didn't do right."

The teacher felt a tug on his shirt and looked down. Philip was standing beside him. "It's mine," Philip said. "It's mine."

And the children said, "You don't ever do things right, Philip. There's nothing there!"

"I did so do it," Philip said. "I did do it. It's empty. The tomb is empty!"

There was silence, a full silence. And for you people who don't believe in miracles, I want to tell you that one happened that day last spring. From that time on, it was different. Philip suddenly became a part of that group of eight-year-old children. They took him in. He was set free from the tomb of his differentness.

Philip died last summer. His family had known since the time that he was born that he wouldn't live out a full life span. Many other things had been wrong with his tiny little body. And so, late last July, with an infection that most normal children could have quickly shrugged off, Philip died. The mystery simply enveloped him.

He was buried from that church. And on that day at the funeral, nine eight-year-old children marched right up to the altar, not with flowers to cover over the stark reality of death. Nine eight-year-olds, with their Sunday school teacher, marched right up to that altar, and laid on it an empty egg—an empty, old discarded pantyhose egg. □

The Pastor and Lent and Easter

● by D-B Heusser

For the early church the Easter experience was the focal point of its mission and teaching ministry. Though it still is a very important part of our ministry, I feel that it has been replaced in many of our churches by Christmas as the key season of the Christian year.

Lent is often the object of many jokes, especially in relationship to giving up something. Lent, though, is an important and serious time, a time of spiritual preparation for Good Friday and Easter. It is a time for each person to become prepared to understand, experience, and respond to the meaning of the death and resurrection of Christ Jesus.

This year I would like to explore some possible ways we can help make the time of Lent and Easter a meaningful and growing experience in the life of our membership.

Some possible ways that we as pastors might help are:

1. *Teacher Assistance.* Lent and Easter are not just one day. Lent is a season of forty days. During this period church school classes are usually studying many of the concepts of Easter. Often teachers need some background help so that their teaching may be more theologically effective.

● You might wish to have a series of meetings with teachers to look at and discuss their curriculum resources. See if the teachers have any questions about what they are being called upon to share.

● As the pastor you might review the various curriculum resources. Identify the key themes, Scriptures, and ideas. You could then preach a series of sermons from these themes and Scriptures during the Lenten season.

● Use a newsletter, teacher discussion, or sermons to deal with some of the theological concepts of Easter (i.e., redemption, salvation, life, hope, death, new life, and incarnation).

2. *Devotional Book.* Ask the members of the congregation to write brief devotional thoughts to be included in a Lenten/Easter devotional book. This book would be distributed on Ash Wednesday and used by the members of the congregation in their spiritual preparation and thought. Some possible topics could be: "What Does Easter Mean to Me?" "What Does the Death and Resurrection of Jesus Mean to (for) Me?"

3. *Lenten/Easter Nights.* These would be a series of special nights to provide a variety of learning experiences. Some would be for study, others would be for fun, and still others for a serious time together. Some possible ideas:

● *Learning Center Night.* Have a number of learning centers set up for children, youth, and adults. Ask persons to visit three or more in the hour's time. The National Teacher Education Project has an excellent series of Lenten/Easter learning centers already set up for children, youth, and adults. You can order from N.T.E.P., 7214 E. Granada Rd., Scottsdale, AZ 85257. Or you may wish to use the ideas suggested in the article "Pancakes, Pretzels, and Possibilities for Lent" found on page 14.

● *Film Night.* Show a Lenten/Easter film or filmstrip and have a discussion following. Some possible films or filmstrips are: *Alive, The Investigation, It's About This Carpenter* (available from American Baptist Films). Remember, the important point is not the film or filmstrip, but the discussion which follows! This is where real learning will take place.

● *Banner Night.* As a group, design and make some banners for classrooms, social hall, or sanctuary. Consider a series of banners dealing with the life and suffering of Christ for the Lenten time and a series dealing with life and the resurrection for Easter.

● *Seder Meal.* Experience the meal that Jesus and the disciples were celebrating at the Lord's Supper. Share together the Seder, perhaps on Maundy Thursday.

● *Make-a-Gift Night.* Make some gifts to be given to shut-ins. Possible gifts: Easter cards or bookmarks or small banners with the symbols of Easter.

These are just a few brief ideas which may help your thinking and planning for Lent and Easter.

The time is now short! Call together a committee and brainstorm ideas to make Lent a time of meaningful preparation for Easter. *Begin now!* □

The Reverend D-B Heusser is Pastor of the Fowler Baptist Church of Fowler, California.

A Lenten Triad
Lenten and Easter devotional activities for the home
● by Marjorie Lundeen

How to Use This Article

This article contains ideas for one home worship service each week of Lent and for a home Easter celebration. If you already have daily devotions privately or as a family, you will want to continue that. Use the ideas in this article for one home worship time each week. Involve everyone who lives with you.

Lent is usually thought of as a somber, reflective time. This mood is proper because Lent reminds us of the forty days Jesus spent in the wilderness fasting and praying. We should take time to meditate during Lent. However, the Sundays are not included in the forty days of Lent because on Sundays we celebrate Christ's resurrection. It is appropriate during Lent to have home worship experiences that are joyful as well as somber.

As you plan your worship experiences, you need not worship the same day or time every week. Look over the ideas and adapt them to your tastes and interests. Scripture references and prayers are included. Vary the order of your worship. Try to use various translations of the Bible. And sometimes make up your own prayers. Find ways to make meaningful the lighting and extinguishing of the candles of your Lenten triad.

Try to create experiences that might become traditions in your home. Lent and Easter can be as rich in meaning and significance as Advent and Christmas—perhaps even more. Pray for God's presence in your home. May these new experiences bring many blessings to you!

Editor's Note

The ideas in this article were written primarily for home use. However, they may be adapted for church school or church worship.

Reprinted from a booklet published for The American Lutheran Church Women. Copyright © 1977 Augsburg Publishing House. Used by permission.

Making a Lenten Triad

Before Lent begins—or during the first week of Lent—make a Lenten triad to be used as the focus of your worship at home. Make a triangular base from three wooden strips, such as those used for the sides of a picture frame, or you might use a triangle of thick Styrofoam. Make holes or use nails for six candles, two on each side of the triangle. Insert six purple candles. Place a single white candle in the middle of the triad.

Make the triad uniquely yours as you decorate it for each worship event. You might use ribbons or flowers, or various colors of fabric as drapes. Perhaps on Good Friday you will use a black drape or lay thorny branches on the triad.

The triad will be used throughout Lent to remind us of Jesus' pending death. The white candle, although unlit, will represent the promise of the resurrection. During the first week's service, all six purple candles will be lighted. Each successive week the triad is used, one candle will be extinguished. After Good Friday, the triad should remain dark until Easter when the white candle will be lighted.

Week 1
LENT—A CALL TO DISCIPLESHIP

Things to do
- Make the Lenten triad if you haven't already done so.

Light six candles.

Scripture: Hebrews 12:7-11

Things to talk about
- The symbolism of the triad.
- Your commitment to Christ.
- The discipline spoken of in the Scripture portion.

Traditions to consider
- Having daily personal devotions during Lent, using *The Secret Place* or some other devotional aid.
- Buying a new Bible, a hymnal, a Bible storybook, a Bible atlas, a Bible dictionary, novel, or some other book on birthdays or anniversaries.
- Buying a book to give to your church library.
- Observing fast days during Lent, perhaps with sacrificial giving for relief of world hunger.

Things to pray about
- The ability to learn from discipline.
- Faithfulness to your commitment to Christ.

A closing prayer

Lord, Lent can be a depressing time. Winter drags on, and we long for spring. Help us to use Lent as a time of disciplined reflection. Teach us something of Christ's obedience. Remind us that Lent leads to Easter and that we are preparing for a great celebration. Amen.

Week 2
LENT—A TIME TO PRAY

Things to do
- Write new prayers for your home for morning, bedtime, and meals.
- Make prayer reminders to hang up in your home.

Light five candles.

Scripture: Philippians 4:4-7

Things to talk about
- Worries in your home.
- Prayers that have been answered.
- How you can find joy in every situation.
- What you can thank God for.

Traditions to consider
- Setting aside specific times for daily prayer.
- Holding hands with friends and family members during table grace.
- Kneeling to pray in your home.

Things to pray about
- Worries you have talked about.
- The things you are thankful for.
- Learning how to pray.

A closing prayer

Heavenly Father, remind us of the power of prayer. We know it can change lives and work miracles. We want to remember to pray when we are confident as well as when we are worried. Help us to pray our own thoughts, not just the words of others. Hear our prayers, O Lord. Amen.

Week 3
LENT—A REASON TO GIVE THANKS

Things to do
- Find a reason to celebrate in your home this week—a birthday, an anniversary, good health, success, friendship, a new purchase, or gratitude. Have a party or a special meal.
- Make some Easter decorations for your home. Remember that the butterfly is an Easter symbol.

Light four candles.

Scripture: Colossians 3:12-17

Things to talk about
- The example Jesus gave us for the way we ought to live.

- The importance of being thankful.
- What you are thankful for.

Traditions to consider
- Telling God each evening what you appreciated about the day.
- Giving a book to your church library each year in the spirit of celebration.
- Writing thank-you notes to people who might not expect them.

Things to pray about
- What Jesus has done for us.
- Things you are thankful for.
- People who need to know about God's love.

A closing prayer

Yes, God, Lent is a time to be thankful. We thank you for our many blessings, the things we often take for granted. We thank you, too, for our troubles, for we know they help us to grow. Thank you most of all for the gift of your Son, for in his life, death, and resurrection we have been set free. Amen.

Week 4
LENT—A PAUSE TO REMEMBER

Things to do
- Thank God that every day you can talk and walk with God as his child.
- Get out old photo albums and reminisce about special events in your life.
- Write out your family tree.

Light three candles.

Scripture: Deuteronomy 11:13-21

Things to talk about
- Your daily relationship to God.
- Special events in your life—use pictures, if you wish.
- Your family background.

Traditions to consider
- Reviving some customs from your ancestral heritage.
- Commemorating your ancestry through a recipe, a decoration, or litany.

Things to pray about
- Your relationship with God.
- Things to thank God for in your life.
- Your family and others who have influenced you.

A closing prayer

Father, we thank you for the people and events that have influenced us. Help us to remember and appreciate our cultural heritage. Even more, remind us that we are part of the family of God. That is our greatest inheritance. Amen.

Week 5
LENT—A CHANCE TO GROW

Things to do
- Plant something in your home or yard.

- If you have houseplants, bring several together in one spot. Clean the leaves, water, fertilize, and do necessary pruning and repotting.
- Each time you care for living things in your home and yard, think about your own spiritual growth.

Light two candles.

Scripture: Luke 8:11-15

Things to talk about
- The parable of the sower.
- The elements needed for growth as a Christian.
- The things that keep us from growing spiritually.

Traditions to consider
- Buying an Easter lily for your home and/or for someone else.
- Fasting one meal or day a week or eating a simple meal during Lent and giving the money saved to someone in need of food.

Things to pray about
- Thank God that you are growing in your Christian life.
- That God will help you be faithful in reading and enjoying his Word.
- The things that keep us from growing spiritually.

A closing prayer
God, we thank you that the seed, your Word, has been planted in our hearts. Show us how to weed out the things that would choke it. We will try to cultivate your word in our lives, trusting you to prune and harvest. Amen.

Week 6
LENT—A FACT TO FACE

Things to do
- Spend some time sitting in darkness after the last purple candle on the triad has been extinguished.
- Have a special worship on Good Friday. (See traditions below as a possibility.)

Light one candle.

Scripture: Luke 23:44-49

Things to talk about
- Loved ones who have died.
- Death.
- The Scripture (Luke 23:44–49) and Jesus' dying on the cross.

Traditions to consider
- Remembering a loved one who has died, visiting the cemetery, or dedicating a gift as a memorial.
- Having a service in your home every Good Friday. This is traditionally called a Tenebrae service.

Things to pray about
- Thank Jesus for suffering and dying for us.
- Thank God that the gloom of Good Friday is followed by the joy of Easter.
- Those who have died and for your thankfulness for them.
- Those who are sick and might be facing death.

A closing prayer
God, when we think of death, we feel sad and afraid—sad about the loved ones we have lost, afraid to talk about our own death. We are stunned to think that you let your Son die for our sins. Help us see beyond death to victory, the victory that Easter brings. Amen.

EASTER—A DAY TO REJOICE

Things to do
- Worship in your home at midnight or sunrise.
- Have a special Easter breakfast, perhaps with hot cross buns.
- Give your family and friends folded paper butterflies with their names on them.
- Make a mobile of the butterflies for your home.

Light the white candle.

Scripture: Matthew 28:1-10

Things to talk about
- The experience of Mary Magdalene and the other Mary.
- The meaning of Easter and the resurrection.
- Why butterflies are a symbol of Easter.
- How "go and tell" is a part of the Easter story.

Traditions to consider
- Keeping Easter decorations for decorating your home each year.
- Using a white candle, the symbol of the resurrection, as a focal point for continuing home worship.
- Keeping the triad for use every Lent and Easter.

Things to pray about
- Thank God for Easter and what it means.
- Thank God for your new life because of Easter.
- That God will help you "go and tell."

A closing prayer
Easter has come! Lord, we rejoice that Jesus' tomb is empty. Remind us that that is the most important day of the year, for today our new life can begin. Help us to feel our freedom in the risen Christ. Alleluia! Amen. □

The Lenten Banner

● by Lois A. Glading

Even before Advent was over, our pastor, Dr. Leonard J. Hatch, was thinking about Lent. He asked me to be chairman of a committee to design the morning worship services for Lent at First Baptist Church, Dover, Delaware. Our goals were to have a unifying theme for the six Sundays of Lent and to provide opportunities for more lay participation in the worship services.

Our committee was composed of those who already are responsible for a portion of the morning worship service: choir director, organist, and pastor. Also on the committee were a representative from the board of dea-

cons, an interested church member with artistic ability, and myself. We met in early January for a "Tuesday morning huddle." We considered many ideas. We were struck by the words of Herbert Lockyer: "The very word 'Lent' is filled with the thought of tears and contrition, of vigils and fasts, of prayers and penitence, and of the discipline of earnest religion. In a clear, unmistakable voice Lent says to every believer *remember Jesus Christ*."[1] We desired for our people to think again of the sacrifice of our Lord and to reexamine their com-

Lois A. Glading is Director of Children's Ministry and Pastoral Assistant of the First Baptist Church of Dover, Delaware.

[1] Herbert Lockyer, *The Lenten Sourcebook* (Grand Rapids: Zondervan Publishing House, 1968), p. 7.

mitment to him. Thus, the words "remember Jesus Christ" became our theme.

As a way of visually "remembering Jesus Christ," we purchased directions for "The Lenten Banner" from Contemporary Drama Service.[2] This packet of materials included directions for making a large banner on which eight symbols are attached with Velcro fasteners. Each symbol represented an event in the last week of Jesus'

the congregation brought the symbol to the chancel area. One family member placed the symbol on the banner, as the other family members read the short script describing the event represented by the symbol. Since we have two morning worship services, fifteen families participated in "The Lenten Banner."

Our working outline, as developed by our pastor, was as follows:

Remember Jesus Christ

	Symbol	Sermon Title	Scripture	Theme
First Sunday of Lent	Rooster	Remembering His Forgiveness	Matthew 26:31-35; 69-75	Christ's forgiveness of Peter in spite of his denial
Second Sunday of Lent	Towel and Basin	Remembering His Example	John 13:1-17	Following Christ's example by serving others
Third Sunday of Lent	Gavel	Remembering His Trial	John 18:28–19:16	Trial before Pilate
Fourth Sunday of Lent	Dice	Remembering His Humiliation	John 19:23-30	Soldiers gambling at the cross; rejection of Jesus
Fifth Sunday of Lent	Crown of Thorns	Remembering His Suffering	Matthew 27:27-54	His crucifixion
Sixth Sunday of Lent (Palm Sunday)	Palm Branch	Remembering His Triumph	Mark 11:1-11	His triumphal entry
Maundy Thursday	Chalice and Wafer	Remembering His Sacrifice	Various Scriptures	Communion service of remembrance
Easter Day	Easter Lily	Remembering His Resurrection	John 20:1-10	Celebration of new life

life. A symbol was to be placed on the banner on each of the six Sundays of Lent and on Maundy Thursday and Good Friday. Also included were eight short scripts. Each script briefly told about one event of that week, which was represented by a symbol.

We adapted this material to fit our own situation. Our banner was a horizontal one, rather than vertical, so that it could be hung in the chancel area of the sanctuary; the order of two of the symbols was reversed. We do not have a Good Friday service; therefore, we deleted that symbol and added a symbol and script for Easter. Our banner, including the symbols, was made by the artistic member of our committee.

Our pastor coordinated his sermon topics with the symbol for each week. The morning Scripture also retold the event associated with the symbol. And, as much as possible, the hymns and choral anthems reinforced the symbol.

In the early part of the worship service, a family from

What was the response of the congregation to "The Lenten Banner"? We heard many favorable comments, particularly about the different parts of the worship service being coordinated with the banner symbol for the day. There was also a sense of anticipation as people wondered what the next symbol would be. We were surprised to find that people in the community, who do not attend First Baptist, had heard about "The Lenten Banner" and were making comments and asking questions about it.

The families who participated in "The Lenten Banner" took their responsibility very seriously. They rehearsed at home, and some families also practiced in the sanctuary. Because of their active involvement in the worship service, each family gained a deeper appreciation for the meaning of the events surrounding Christ's death and resurrection.

This Lenten experience was a very meaningful one for our congregation as we "remembered Jesus Christ" through visual symbols, Scripture, music, and the spoken word. Especially significant was seeing families of all ages actively leading in the worship experience! □

[2]Contemporary Drama Service, Box 457, 1529 Brook Drive, Downers Grove, IL 60515.

Pancakes, Pretzels, and Possibilities for Lent

● by Martha and Paul Osborne

Pancakes? Pretzels? Lent? What do these have in common? And why are Christians talking about them?

Traditionally the Christian church has viewed the season of Lent as a time of personal and corporate preparation for the celebraton of Easter. Many Christians are finding traditional Lenten practices to be helpful in developing a personal view of Christ's forty days in the wilderness. By connecting with the church through the ages and by developing new Lenten traditions, it may be possible for Christians to encounter new meanings in the yearly celebration for Easter.

In our own congregation, enthusiasm has grown for observing Advent as the time to prepare for Christmas, but Lent is still approached with little understanding.

As we undertook the task of educating our congregation and possibly creating some enthusiasm for observing Lent, several questions were raised:

1. How can we develop a Lenten program in our church that includes both children and adults?

2. How can we help people to develop individual and family traditions for Lent?

3. How can we emphasize the Lenten season in the total life of our church?

Considering these issues and the makeup of our congregation, we chose to begin our task with an intergenerational event to explore the various aspects of Lent through learning experiences, creative activities, fellowship, and worship. Shrove Tuesday, the traditional day for cleaning out the pantry in readiness for the Lenten fast, became the focus for our design.

Meals have proved to be successful in bringing our members together, so we planned a pancake supper, another familiar Lenten practice. The evening included four learning centers for children and adults, a craft shop, the supper, and time for sharing during the closing worship.

The following section outlines the event.

Welcome to Our Lenten Pancake Supper!

Tonight you will have an opportunity to learn about Lent through four learning centers and a craft shop before enjoying pancakes, bacon, and fruit for supper. We shall end our evening together with a short time of worship.

Martha Osborne is the director of Christian education at Second Presbyterian Church, 13 North Fifth Street, Richmond, Virginia 23219.
Paul Osborne is a grades 1-6 teacher of Bible at St. Catherine's School in Richmond.

Reprinted by permission from *Alert*, November, 1979.

Attention, All Children!

This is a time for children and adults to learn together. Please work with your parent or another adult at all times.

Getting Started

Read the descriptions of all four centers and then choose one with which to begin your study of Lent.

The Learning Centers
I. Why Do We Celebrate Lent?

A. Purpose: This center explores the general Lenten season and its scriptural parallels through taped Scripture readings, resource materials, and Lenten calendars. This center is designed for ages eight through adult.

B. Activities for working alone or in small groups

1. Listen to the taped account of Jesus' forty days in the wilderness from *Luke 4:1-13*. You may want to follow the text, using one of the Bibles provided. The questions at the end of the account may help direct your thinking or provide discussion material for your group.

2. Read the selections from resources provided about the church year; check your knowledge of these traditions by conversation with another person.

3. Take some time to look at a Lenten calendar. Blank calendars provided are for scheduling special activities and events for your own observance of Lent.

C. Resources

1. *The Story of the Christian Year*, by George M. Gibson (Abingdon Press, 1955).

2. *The Year of the Lord*, by Theodore J. Kleinhans (Concordia Publishing House, 1967).

3. "Praise God—Worship Through the Year," by Mary Faith Carson and Arlo D. Duba, in *Concern*, Spring, 1979.

4. Copies of several versions of the Bible.

II. What Are the Special Days of Lent?

A. Purpose: This center focuses on Ash Wednesday, Palm Sunday, Maundy Thursday, Good Friday, and Easter Day. Traditions about and meanings of these days are explored through games and other resources. This center provides ideas for home celebration of Lent for ages five through adult.

B. Activities for learning about the days of Lent

1. Play the "Days of Lent" game with several other people.

2. Read the Information Cards.

3. Work the "Days of Lent" crossword puzzle.

4. Plan projects for yourself or for your family.

C. Resources

1. Crossword puzzle (page 16).

2. Write to the authors for the "Days of Lent" game.

3. Information Cards are made from materials and information in *Teaching and Celebrating Lent and Easter* (Griggs Educational Service, 1731 Barcelona Street, Livermore, CA 94550).

III. What Are the Symbols of Lent?

A. Purpose: This center explores the traditional and contemporary symbols of Lent. Resources and activities show how these symbols may be used to enhance personal celebration and corporate worship during Lent.

B. Activities for learning about symbols of Lent

1. Use the puzzle cards to match symbols and meanings.

2. Use the matching quiz to review your knowledge of Lenten symbols.

3. Have available in the craft shop materials and instructions for making practical and decorative items using symbols of the Lenten season.

C. Resources

1. *Lilies, Rabbits, and Painted Eggs: The Story of the Easter Symbols,* by Edna Barth (The Seabury Press, Inc., 1970).

2. *Young Readers Book of Christian Symbolism,* by Michael Daves (Abingdon Press, 1967).

3. Puzzle cards and matching quiz (page 16).

IV. How Can I Observe Lent?

A. Purpose: This center focuses on personal reflection and preparation during the season of Lent. It is a resource center for youth and adults.

B. Activities for learning ways to observe Lent

1. Read one or more of the Bible passages describing experiences in the wilderness: *Luke 4:1-13; Exodus 24:12-18; I Kings 19:1-18.*

2. Read the discussion on *Luke 4:1-13* in one of the commentaries.

3. Read selections from *Out of Solitude,* by Henri J. Nouwen (Ave Maria Press, 1974).

4. Use the materials provided here (or a calendar from the first center) to design a reading scheme for yourself that will take you through the Lenten season.

5. Please share ideas or resources for this center on the posted sheet for listing of resources.

C. Resources: Display resources available from the church library or borrowed from a local bookstore.

V. The Craft Shop

A. Purpose: After the symbols of Lent have been studied and activities for observing the special days have been selected, the craft shop provides materials and instructions for trying out ideas in various art forms and craft projects.

B. Activities

1. Sponge-print place mats with symbols for use at meals on special days during Lent.

2. Create greeting cards, stationery, and bookmarks with Lenten symbols and messages.

3. Design centerpieces or banners with butterflies, flowers, and other symbols.

4. Construct clay pretzels as symbols of the Lenten fast.

5. Start seedlings to sprout by Easter as symbols of new life.

A Time for Sharing

While most of the participants were working in the learning centers, several adults and young people were busy in the kitchen preparing pancakes for supper. After an hour of concentrated study and creative activities, the tempting smell of pancakes hot off the griddle was the signal that it was suppertime! Even the youngest children joined us for supper—eating pancakes proved to be a truly intergenerational event. After supper, we shifted our chairs to form a semicircle and prepared for the closing time of sharing and worship.

We began our time of worship by viewing the opening portion of *Why We Celebrate Holy Week,** an excellent filmstrip depicting Luke's account of Jesus' temptation in the wilderness and the Holy Week events. After seeing the filmstrip, participants were asked to share in small groups their answers to the following questions:

1. What is Lent all about?

2. Why is it important to the church?

3. What are some ways to observe the season individually or with others?

After sharing some of our discoveries about Lenten traditions and some of our own plans for Easter preparation, we closed our time of learning and fellowship with prayer, song, and a new awareness of the pancakes, pretzels, and possibilities for Lent.

The Evaluation

Our Lenten pancake supper was planned as an intergenerational event to be a first step in educating the congregation about the Lenten season. What we saw and heard as the evening progressed led us to conclude that our purpose was accomplished. We saw children and adults working together and heard them talking to one another about discoveries they were making about the symbols of Lent and the special days. Adults and young persons together prepared pancakes to feed seventy people. Enthusiastic comments from children and adults indicated that a Lenten pancake supper could easily become a tradition for our church.

Another indication of the success of the event came when church school teachers continued to use many of the learning center activities in their Sunday morning classes. Those involved in planning and implementing the program also decided that more opportunities for all ages to study, learn, and worship together should be offered. □

*Available from Griggs Educational Service. See address under II.C.3.

Days of Lent
Crossword (For Center II, Activity 3)

Down
1. Holy Thursday is also called _____ _____.
2. The day we celebrate Jesus' resurrection is _____.
3. 6. At Communion we have _____ and _____.
4. The day we celebrate Jesus' triumphal entry into Jerusalem is _____ _____.
6. See 3 Down.
11. On Easter we say, "Hallelujah! Christ is _____!"

Across
5. The day on which Lent begins is _____ _____.
7. The name of the forty days and six Sundays before Easter is _____.
8. We call the meal that Jesus and his disciples had on the Thursday before Easter the Last _____.
9. The Jewish feast that Jesus was celebrating with his disciples was _____.
10. The day we remember especially for Jesus' suffering and death on the cross is _____ _____.

Puzzle Cards (For Center III, Activity 1)

To make puzzle cards:
Cut rectangles of stiff cardboard (a mat knife is good for cutting clean edges). Use the symbols from the matching quiz. Write the name of the symbol and draw or paste a picture of it on the top portion of the card. Write the definition at the bottom and put the number midway near the edge. Cut the card in half in any puzzle pattern.

Instructions
1. Match the symbol to its meaning by fitting the puzzle cards together.
2. As you match the cards, read the meanings aloud.
3. When you have completed the cards, check yourself by taking the matching quiz.

Matching Quiz (For Center III, Activity 2)

1. Match the symbol with its meaning, writing the symbol number on the line beside the correct meaning.
2. Check your answers with the puzzle cards game.
3. If you need a review, play the puzzle cards game again.

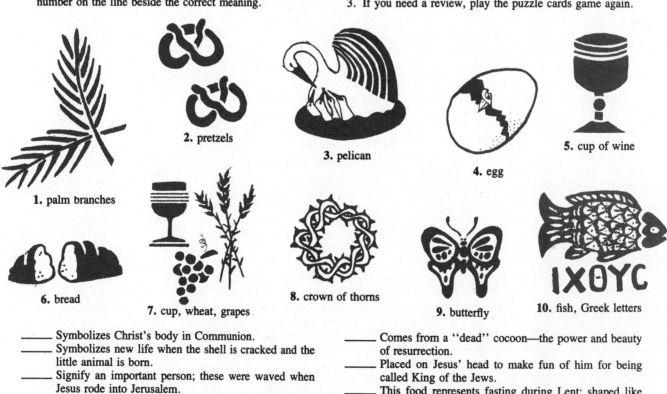

1. palm branches
2. pretzels
3. pelican
4. egg
5. cup of wine
6. bread
7. cup, wheat, grapes
8. crown of thorns
9. butterfly
10. fish, Greek letters

_____ Symbolizes Christ's body in Communion.
_____ Symbolizes new life when the shell is cracked and the little animal is born.
_____ Signify an important person; these were waved when Jesus rode into Jerusalem.
_____ Letters of the first symbol for Christians. Jesus Christ, Son of God, Savior.
_____ Three symbols together meaning the Last Supper.

_____ Comes from a "dead" cocoon—the power and beauty of resurrection.
_____ Placed on Jesus' head to make fun of him for being called King of the Jews.
_____ This food represents fasting during Lent; shaped like arms folded in prayer.
_____ This bird gives up her life to save her young.
_____ Symbolizes Christ's blood in Communion.

Young Children Produce a Lenten Newspaper
• by Marie E. Cross

As a Lenten program the Christian education committee of a church in Anchorage, Kentucky, came up with a "newspaper program" for all students of kindergarten through grade 6. We produced THE LENTEN HERALD.

It was a five-week program, held every Thursday evening. The whole church family gathered for worship at 6 P.M., followed by a potluck supper at 6:30 P.M. and an hour-long study for all ages.

Our topic, or theme, for the newspaper program was Holy Week. The first evening was spent just introducing Lent and its position in the church year and the days of Holy Week. Subsequent weeks were spent dealing with the particular days and events.

Each evening, after supper, all the boys and girls gathered to view a filmstrip that introduced the ideas or events to be studied in that session. One time, the children interviewed a person playing the role of the apostle Peter—to get another perspective on the events of Holy Week and the ministry of Jesus. They really got involved in this procedure.

After the filmstrip, the children were divided into groups: kindergarten, grades 1-2, grades 3-4, and grades 5-6, in four separate rooms, with a team of teachers for each group.

In the classroom they continued the discussion of the filmstrip and related materials. Then they transferred what they were learning into "articles" for THE LENTEN HERALD—drawings, puzzles, reviews, and the like.

We used a spirit duplicator. The students could use the purple masters for drawing and writing, and these could easily be passed from one person to the next. Everyone contributed something to the newspaper each evening; so it was always the product of the entire group. We were always running out of time, but it was an exciting experience for all the boys and girls.

One of the extra benefits was the time shared in learning and planning among the teachers. Every Sunday after morning worship and church school, the Lenten teachers and two Christian education committee members met for an hour to plan the coming Thursday's lessons. Resource materials and a preview of the filmstrip for that week helped each teacher to plan for his/her age level. Then, of course, we always got into a discussion of the material at our level, too.

Here's a sample from THE LENTEN HERALD (a page from grades 1-2):

> "Today I heard a robin sing,
> Now I know it will soon be spring.
> The little flowers are peeking through,
> Some are yellow, some are blue.
> All these things I like to see—
> They make me glad as I can be!
> Happy Easter!"   □

Multimedia on Palm Sunday

● by Chris K. Eng

In an instant the room was pitch dark. Suddenly, a child's face appeared, filling the entire movie screen. Her voice captured the people's attention as they listened to what she had to say. The music playing in the background seemed to drive her point home.

Instead of the local movie theater, this was happening in a church sanctuary. The season was Easter. When the show was over, the people realized that they would not soon forget the impact of this multimedia presentation.

The church lives in an electronic age. Ideas, feelings, and messages are imprinted on the mind's memory not just with words but also with colored pictures, captivating sound waves, and powerful images. The teaching that is done must somehow lend itself to creating an experience which in and of itself has the potential to bring about a change in attitudes.

A Multimedia Easter

When I first thought about assembling the elements to a traditional Easter program, my inclinations leaned towards the typical prepackaged commodity available at any Christian bookstore or music center. But last year I wondered what impact would be felt if that program were produced at home. With sufficient involvement by various youth a live learning experience could come out of the production itself. It was worth a try.

The idea was not new. But gathering the ingredients of a multimedia project, which I usually reserve for those fortunate churches that are blessed with enough electronic machinery and skilled talent to pull off such a monumental job, for my own church was. The fear of the work involved had kept me from experimenting, but this time something inside compelled me to take a leap of faith. So I decided to "go for it"!

As I arranged a job description of the tasks to be done, three areas became evident. First, I needed to state the goals I wanted to accomplish or the effects I intended to have. Second, I needed to put forth some specific strategies or the means by which I could fulfill these goals. Third, I needed to find the individuals who could provide the resources to complete the project.

The primary goal was to let children and youth com-

municate their meaning of Easter. If these persons could be helped to articulate the Passion story and the great love of God in the person of Jesus of Nazareth, then the effort made in this project would be more than worth the actual costs incurred. The powerful message as fleshed out in these individuals could be documented by studies which affirm the influence of children and youth on their peers, their parents, and other adults.

I next developed my strategies which stated the specific things to be done and the equipment to be secured. The children and youth needed to be interviewed; good slides needed to be taken; and the final compilation of slides, interviews, and background music had to be worked out. The checklist of equipment included two or three tape recorders with tone control, an SLR camera with zoom lens (preferably 80-200mm), slide film with high ASA rating (200 to 400), cassette tapes, commercially taped music, slide projector, movie screen, hook-up jacks, and a good public address system.

Finding those persons within the church who could enable the doing of this project was very important. In my congregation I looked for persons who were gifted in this manner. I found that involving junior high and senior high youth was a learning ministry in itself. Since I found myself with many inexperienced individuals, I trained them in interviewing, photography, and program development. The real art was required when I finally had the raw data to put everything into a coherent whole.

Several months before Easter, I began to prepare the teachers and their classes for the oncoming interruptions. Pictures for slides would be shot over a period of four Sundays. While pictures were being taken, children and youth from each of the classes would be interviewed privately. Volunteers would be solicited. Time would be allotted for retakes if slides or interviews did not turn out as anticipated. The real challenge would be to balance the tendency for some children and youth to be shy and withdrawn with those who were very active and outspoken. With enough patience we would eventually be able to get the kind of material we wished.

Helps

Action shots are helpful. Slides should be taken of faces or profiles. Spontaneity and naturalness should be sought for in both closeups and action shots. It is im-

When the author wrote this article, he was Associate Pastor at the Japanese Baptist Church, Seattle, Washington. He is now pastoring at the Nuuanu Congregational Church, Honolulu, Hawaii.

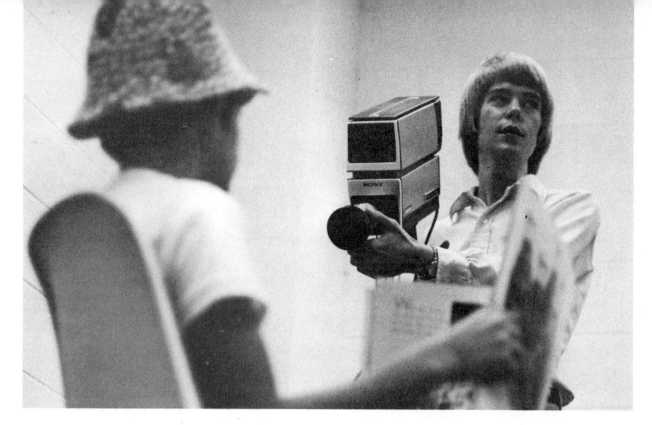

portant that the subject or action fill the entire lens. Photos of the church facilities and other subjects can be taken in conjunction with the overall plan.

A quiet place is needed to tape-record the interviews. A recorder with tone control is very helpful. A high quality tape cassette must be used since the interviews will later be recorded onto the master tape. It is helpful to have the questions that will be asked written out so the student can see what will be asked. The format could run like this: "Hello, my name is _____. Easter means to me _____." Periodically check the taping quality to insure consistent and adequate volume and clarity.

The typical Carousel slide tray holds eighty slides. I found that shooting at least twice that many photos guaranteed that I had the ones I wanted. For Easter, shots of bunnies, chocolate candy, and decorated eggs were important. Commercial slides are available of scenes of the Holy Land and of Christ's Passion. The subtle blend of secular and religious can provide a very powerful effect.

One idea that seemed useful is the "focusing in" effect. You can start with slides of the world and then focus down to our nation, the state, your local community, and your church. Or you could start with the adults of your congregation and move down through the various age groups until you zero in on children. Likewise, the secular theme of Easter bunnies and candy can pave the way for the real meaning of Lent in the events of Good Friday and Easter.

The background music should be arranged to bring home some of the rich emotions and feelings that you are trying to communicate. Again, you can artistically blend secular music and religious music.

Putting It All Together

The mechanics of putting it all together can be fun and entertaining. Once all the basic materials have been col-lected, you can spend an afternoon and evening at the church assembling the heart of the program. It is especially helpful if you can locate a writer who can provide the basic structure for your production. Then you should look for an individual who is good at sorting through slides. The real task is to assemble the slides, interviews, and background music in such a way that they all flow naturally and yet powerfully. Once the final slides are arranged in the Carousel tray and the master tape is made, you should run through the entire program several times to work out the bugs and make changes as necessary. It is helpful if you can plug your cassette tape recorder into the public address system in your sanctuary if you are having the multimedia program in your church. The newer models of slide projectors allow you to program the slide changes automatically.

The time and money put into this endeavor will earn high dividends. Usually the costs will be low in comparison with purchased products. The production I did for our Palm Sunday program ran around thirty-five dollars for film, developing, and tapes.

The final product can be reused or placed in your resource file for future projects. Before long you will be amazed at how adept and skilled you become. You'll have a wealth of slides from which you can pick and choose in creating almost any kind of effect for special occasions like birthdays, anniversaries, and other events in the life of the church.

With enough creativity and involvement you'll soon have the essential ingredients for a successful ministry. For not only will the lives of these children, youth, and their parents be affected by the production but also the lives of the persons who were committed to assembling the final product will be touched. The use of media in teaching and learning can be a powerful tool in a world where electronics is the name of the game. □

What You Have Always Wanted to Know About Easter

● by Martha Brown

Do you know what the complicated formula is that decides when Easter comes?

It is the first Sunday, after the first full moon, after the vernal equinox. *Vernal equinox* means the day in the spring when the days and nights are again of equal length. It is the first day of spring.

Have you ever thought about the significance of that formula?

When we think of it in terms of light, it can have a beautiful, symbolic meaning. The ancients were much more aware of the effects of the moon and sun and light and darkness than they were of months and dates and calendars. The shortest day of the year is December 21. Just when it might look as if darkness is growing and will overtake all light, light returns and begins to push back the darkness. In Jesus' birth a new form of light came into our world, and December 25 was chosen to celebrate that event. In the days following the vernal equinox on March 21 there are more hours of light than there are of dark. What better time is there to choose to celebrate Christ's victory over all the dark things this earth could offer—even death itself—than the Sunday after the first full moon (when night itself is at its brightest) after the vernal equinox!

But didn't the early Christians just adopt an already established pagan spring fertility festival and incorporate it into their religion?

The answer here is both yes and no. The very word *Easter* comes from the name of Eostre, who was a Teutonic goddess of spring. When everyone around was celebrating a pagan spring festival that heralded the renewal of life with the coming of a new spring, the early Christians added a spiritual dimension. Newness of life was more than blossoms, leaves, new lambs, and birds. It included the new life of the spirit that they had come to know through the life, death, and resurrection of Jesus. It was as if to say, Yes, the miracle of spring is worthy of our praise and worship, but there's so much more. There's a whole new understanding of "new life" . . . the spirit of Christ lives within us!

Where did Lent come from and what does it mean?

The word itself comes from the Middle English word *lente* and the Old English word *lengten,* meaning *spring.* Lent has been set aside as a time of preparation and remembering. The first Lent lasted forty hours as a reminder of the time Jesus' body lay in the tomb. But in the sixth century Gregory the Great set aside a forty-day period of fasting, penitence, and prayer.

Why are Sundays not included in the time set aside for Lent?

Many people are confused by the forty days because Lent seems to begin more than forty days before Easter. The trick is, you see, that Sundays are not counted because all Sundays are feast days and never fast days.

To understand this, we have to remind ourselves of the reason we worship on Sunday. The original day of worship in the Jewish-Christian heritage was the sabbath—Saturday. This practice goes back to the story of the creation and the resting on the seventh day of the week. After the resurrection of Christ on the *first* day of the week, the early church decided to celebrate in worship the most important event in its Christian heritage. Each Sunday became a time to remember Christ's resurrection on the first day of the week, and, therefore, a happy day, celebration day, feast day, "little Easter" day. So Sunday takes precedence over the Lenten season, and Sundays are not counted in determining the forty days of Lent.

But why forty days?

There could be several reasons. The Israelites, after being freed from bondage in Egypt, wandered with Moses for forty years in the wilderness before coming to the Promised Land. Also, after his baptism Jesus spent forty days alone in spiritual preparation for his ministry and the coming of that first Easter.

This article first appeared in *Through Centenary Windows* newsletters (March 3–24, 1977) for Centenary United Methodist Church, Winston-Salem, North Carolina. Reprinted by permission.

Do all Christians believe in giving something up during Lent?

Some do, some don't. Those who follow this practice believe it will help them remember Jesus every time they deny themselves. The money that would have been spent on the item given up is set aside by some for a special project of helping others.

How did Ash Wednesday get its name?

Many primitive religions, including the early Hebrew religion, felt they could make peace with a god who was angry with them for some wrongdoing by burning a sacrifice. They thought the rising smoke and the odors could reach the dwelling place of the gods. The ashes were the remnants of the offering. Placing ashes on their body showed others that they were sorrowful and trying to renew relations with their god. Lent has come down to us as a time to think about our relationship with God and be appropriately penitent. Some Roman Catholic churches still follow the custom of burning the palms from the previous Palm Sunday and with the ashes making a cross on the forehead of each worshiper. Ash Wednesday is the first day of Lent.

Is it true that Mardi Gras is connected with the celebration of Easter?

Yes. Mardi Gras, when translated from the French, means *Fat Tuesday*. It seems that not every Christian has been excited about entering the Lenten season of fasting and self-reflection that begins with Ash Wednesday. So, on the Tuesday prior to Ash Wednesday, a "last fling" was planned. Practically speaking, this was a good opportunity to use up the last of the meat products that would not be allowed during the fast period.

And spring housecleaning?

Even spring housecleaning can be traced to the cleansing of the household of all traces of meat and meat by-products in accord with the ancient, strict rules of the fast. There were also overtones of making ready for the newness of life in the spring. So the house and all the cooking utensils were cleansed and prepared for a new season as a part of the renewal and readiness to start afresh at Eastertime.

Why do local bakeries sell hot cross buns during Lent?

The spicy, fruit-filled buns became popular as a breakfast treat during the time that meat and eggs were not allowed. The marking of the cross is an additional reminder of the season. Many families bake hot cross buns together as part of their Easter tradition.

Would it surprise you to know that even *pretzels* were developed in Germany to be eaten on fast days? They were made of only flour, salt, and water and were shaped in the form of arms folded in prayer.

What is the origin of the Easter egg?

Ancient civilizations thought of the egg as holding the secret of new life. In India and Egypt, the world was said to have begun by the splitting of a huge egg, one-half becoming the heavens, and the other half becoming the earth. The early Christians converted the pagan custom into a Christian one. Eggs still symbolize the secret of new life—the spiritual new life as found in the life of Christ.

How did a rabbit ever get mixed up in all this?

No one seems to know exactly where or how the "bunny" entered the scene. It seems to have been a spring symbol in several cultures. The rabbit has certainly been the brunt of many jokes because of its association with an abundance of new life. From that perspective, the egg and the rabbit seem to have a lot in common even if nature didn't put them together.

What was the significance of the palms used on Palm Sunday?

At the time of Jesus, palms were a sign of victory. They were often given to the winners of contests of strength or skill. The fulfillment of the Old Testament

prophecy of Zechariah also signified Jesus as the Messiah. "Lo, your king comes to you; triumphant and victorious is he, humble and riding on an ass" (Zechariah 9:9).

Tell me about Maundy Thursday.

On Thursday of Holy Week, Jesus gathered his disciples to share a Passover meal. Passover was the celebration of God's bringing the Hebrew people out of bondage to the Pharaoh of Egypt. Moses had pleaded for their freedom. The Hebrews were told to slay a lamb and place its blood on the doorposts of their homes to avoid the plague that struck the Egyptians. Death "passed over." They were saved by the blood of the lamb. Jesus reinterpreted the meaning of the Passover feast for his disciples in terms of his own ministry. He became the Lamb of God. His body was to be broken and his blood shed. His emphasis changed from the physical salvation the Hebrews experienced in Egypt to a spiritual salvation.

At the meal together, Jesus washed the feet of the disciples and gave them a "new commandment": that they "love one another." The word *Maundy* comes from the Latin *mandatum,* meaning *commandment.* We hear the same root word in the English word *mandate.*

How did Friday ever get the label *Good Friday*?

From the perspective of what man did, it certainly was "bad" Friday; but from the postresurrection perspective of what God did, it can be called "good." Some people explain its origin as a word change from God's Friday to Good Friday. This same change occurs in the English phrase *God be wi' ye* to our modern *good-bye.*

Is it a tradition to eat ham on Easter Sunday?

For some families it seems to be; others have never heard of the tradition. Here again, it can be a dramatic breaking of the Lenten fast. And, also, an unspoken declaration that by Christ's revelation and fulfillment of the law, Christians are no longer bound by Jewish dietary regulations forbidding pork. Lamb is also a favorite dish and can be understood as an important symbol in relation to the life of Christ as the Lamb of God, as the good shepherd, and as a fulfillment of the Old Testament Passover or Paschal lamb.

Where did we get the idea we have to wear new clothes at Eastertime?

As the church grew and developed traditions and customs, Lent became a time to train new members in the faith and baptize them. New white linen clothes were worn for the occasion to symbolize the cleansing and a new life of faith. ☐

Simon of Cyrene

An Easter Play

● **by Irene B. Brand**

The author is a free-lance writer from Point Pleasant, West Virginia.

Cast of Characters

MRS. SELLARDS .... the youth counselor (may be played by a youth)

Teenage girls

LYNN .... quiet and serious

MARIA .... friendly and enthusiastic

VICKIE .... vivacious and argumentative

Teenage boys

ADRIAN .... the tall, athletic type

FITZ .... displays leadership abilities

TROY .... attentive and eager to please

COSTUMING: Mrs. Sellards dresses in casual slacks and blouse. The young people wear jeans and shirts.

PROPERTIES: Mrs. Sellards—Bibles and hymnals; Maria—a pair of shoes.

(Playing time: 20 minutes)

TIME: Thursday of Easter week

PLACE: A church school room or general meeting room of any local church

SETTING: The youth meeting room. There are two entrances, STAGE RIGHT and STAGE LEFT, although one of these entrances may be eliminated if necessary. A table and chair are situated UP RIGHT. Books and literature are placed on the table. About a dozen chairs complete the room's furnishings.

AT RISE: MRS. SELLARDS is alone on stage, arranging chairs in a semicircle UP CENTER and collecting materials for the meeting. LYNN, MARIA, and VICKIE enter STAGE LEFT. MARIA is carrying a package.

VICKIE: Hi, Mrs. Sellards. *(Looking around the room.)* I suppose the boys will be late as usual.

MRS. SELLARDS: Oh, maybe not. We still have a few minutes before seven o'clock.

MARIA *(takes a pair of shoes out of her package):* See my new shoes. They match my Easter dress.

VICKIE *(enviously):* Gee, Maria, they're cool! Mom wouldn't buy any for me. She said I had enough shoes.

LYNN *(to VICKIE):* Don't forget you bought a new pair for the Valentine party. That was only six weeks ago.

MRS. SELLARDS *(handing Bibles and hymnals to the girls):* Will you place these on the chairs, please? We need them for our program tonight.

(ADRIAN, FITZ, and TROY enter STAGE LEFT.)

ADRIAN: Hi, gang! What's new?

VICKIE: You're late, but that isn't news.

ADRIAN *(looking at his watch):* Nope, we aren't late. Are we, Mrs. Sellards?

MRS. SELLARDS *(smiling):* Not much, anyway. Shall we start? I don't think any more of our group will be here tonight. Several families have gone out of town for Easter.

(They sit down, boys on the right of the semicircle, girls on the left. There is an empty chair between them. MRS. SELLARDS sits beside the table.)

MRS. SELLARDS: We'll start our meeting by singing the first verse of "The Old Rugged Cross."

(They open their books and sing.)

MRS. SELLARDS: Lynn, will you give the opening prayer?

(All bow their heads.)

LYNN: Dear Jesus, thank you for dying for us. Thank you for Mrs. Sellards and for the time she takes to be our counselor. Bless everybody, everywhere. Amen. [NOTE: *An original prayer may be substituted if desired.*]

MRS. SELLARDS: I've entitled our program "If I Had Been." I'd like for each of you to name a person connected with the death or resurrection of Jesus and tell why you would like to have been that person. Perhaps we can do a narration on the life of one of the people. Who will begin?

FITZ *(holds up his hand):* I will. If I had been Joseph of Arimathea, I'd have asked for Jesus' body, too. Just think of providing the place for his burial! What a neat way to serve him!

VICKIE: Oh, I don't think that's much for Joseph to do. He was rich as Croesus anyhow, and he was even afraid to tell people that he was a disciple of Jesus. Now, if I had been Mary, I would have stayed with Jesus until the last minute. It wouldn't be easy to watch your son die, but she knelt right there by the cross anyway.

ADRIAN: Well, what about John? He was there, too, and Jesus asked him to take care of Mary. Jesus must have really trusted John to place her in his care.

MARIA: If I had been Salome, or one of the other women who came to anoint his body, I would have purchased the most expensive spices I could find.

LYNN: I wish I had been Mary Magdalene on Easter morning. My feet couldn't have carried me fast enough to spread the news that Jesus was alive.

FITZ: Everybody has mentioned someone except Troy.

ADRIAN: Yeah, man! Speak up.

TROY *(meekly):* I wish I had been Simon of Cyrene.

ADRIAN: Simon of Cyrene! Never heard of him.

VICKIE: Oh, Adrian! He's the one who carried the cross for Jesus.

ADRIAN: That's right. I'd forgotten about him. But I don't think that's much of an idea, Troy. We don't know enough about him to do a narration.

MRS. SELLARDS: Perhaps we should learn something about Simon. We can make-believe what we don't know.

VICKIE *(enthusiastically):* Yes! Let's study Simon of Cyrene.

LYNN: It sounds like an interesting subject to me.

FITZ: Good idea! I'd like to know more about Simon.

ADRIAN: OK. But I think it will be a dud.

MRS. SELLARDS: Look through the Bibles and see what you can learn about Simon. *(They open their Bibles.)*

FITZ: We should start with the Gospels first, I guess. I'll look in Matthew.

MARIA: Let me check Mark.

ADRIAN *(falling into the plan):* I'll see what Luke said about him, and Troy, you should find out if John wrote anything about Simon since it's your idea.

TROY: Sure. I'm willing.

MRS. SELLARDS: The only place you'll find any information is in the closing chapters of the Gospels. That should narrow your search considerably.

(They all turn pages in the Bibles looking for the right Scripture references. Some may check the concordance.)

FITZ: I have it: "And as they came out, they found a man of Cyrene, Simon by name: him they compelled to bear his cross." That's Matthew 27:32.

ADRIAN: Here it is in Luke 23, verse 26: "And as they led him away, they laid hold upon one Simon, a Cyrenian, coming out of the country, and on him they laid the cross, that he might bear it after Jesus."

MARIA: Mark tells a little more about Simon in chapter 15, verse 21: "And they compel one Simon a Cyrenian, who passed by, coming out of the country, the father of Alexander and Rufus, to bear his cross."

LYNN: What have you found, Troy?

TROY: John doesn't even mention his name.

VICKIE: Gee, that isn't much! Is Simon mentioned any other place, Mrs. Sellards?

MRS. SELLARDS: Not that I remember. But let's analyze the information we have about him. What facts did you learn?

MARIA: He was from Cyrene, wherever that is.

MRS. SELLARDS: Does anyone know?

(They all shake their heads, except Fitz.)

FITZ: It's an island in the Mediterranean Sea, I think.

MRS. SELLARDS: No, it was a large merchant city in northern Africa.

ADRIAN: You mean he was an African?

MRS. SELLARDS: Probably not. Doesn't his name give you a clue to his nationality?

TROY: Well, his name was Simon, and there were several people with that name in the New Testament. For instance, Jesus had two disciples called Simon. And I believe I've heard the pastor talk about Simon,

the magician, who was mentioned in the book of Acts.

MRS. SELLARDS: That's right. His name likely indicates that Simon was Jewish. And a large Jewish population lived in Cyrene at that time. He may have been a Jew who had returned to Jerusalem for the Passover, which was a common thing for Jews to do.

VICKIE: So we know where he lived and that he was probably a Jew. *(Looking at the Bible.)* Didn't someone read that he had children?

MARIA: Yes, I did. Mark said that he was the father of Alexander and Rufus. *(She looks at MRS. SELLARDS.)* Did his children become important in Bible times? Do we have any record of their lives?

MRS. SELLARDS: Paul mentioned a man by the name of Rufus in the book of Romans, but we don't know that he was Simon's son.

TROY: Is that enough information for us to act out Simon's story?

FITZ: We can use the facts we have and ad-lib the rest.

After all, we do know how Jesus was treated on the way to his crucifixion. We can imagine the way Simon might have acted.

MRS. SELLARDS: How do you visualize Simon?

ADRIAN: I think he was rich.

VICKIE: He was a classy dresser.

LYNN: He had lots of servants, and it must have been a disgrace for him to carry a cross.

MARIA (excitedly): This is fun. Let's act out the scene. Troy, you wanted to be Simon. Who will play the part of Jesus?

LYNN: Fitz could do a good job.

FITZ (standing up): I'll do it. Maria, you should be Troy's slave.

MARIA: OK.

(MRS. SELLARDS sits quietly, willing that they should assume leadership.)

ADRIAN: I could be a Roman soldier.

MARIA: But what are Lynn and Vickie going to do?

LYNN: We'll be women friends of Jesus who were crying because he had been sentenced to die.

FITZ: Let's begin where the soldiers have beaten Jesus and are sending him to be crucified. Jesus puts the cross on his back and starts toward Calvary.

(The boys prepare to act out the scene DOWN CENTER. FITZ pretends he has the cross on his back and walks slowly, as if the burden is heavy. He stumbles and falls. ADRIAN appears to be whipping FITZ.)

ADRIAN: Get up, swine! You're holding up the rest of the crowd. You'll be late for your own crucifixion. (Laughs as though his remark is a big joke.)

TROY (steps forward; MARIA follows him): Soldier! Leave that poor man alone.

ADRIAN (turning to TROY in surprise): Just who do you think you are, buddy, to be giving orders to a Roman soldier?

TROY (draws himself erect, haughtily): I'm Simon, wealthy merchant from Cyrene, in Jerusalem on business with the Roman governor. I've also come to celebrate the Passover in the city of my ancestors.

ADRIAN: Yeah! Well, I don't care who you are. This man has been condemned to death, and it's up to me to see that he gets to the place of crucifixion.

TROY: But look at him! He has been beaten so badly that his robe is soaked with blood. He isn't able to carry that heavy cross.

ADRIAN (sarcastically): Too bad! I'm not going to carry it for him. If you're so concerned, you carry the cross.

(TROY hesitates, and looks at his clothes, as though he is wearing costly garments; then he pretends to take off his outer coat, which he hands to MARIA.)

TROY: Very well. I'll do it. Slave, carry this garment for me and follow along.

(ADRIAN pantomimes taking the cross and placing it on TROY's back. MARIA helps FITZ to stand, and he moves slowly across stage, with TROY following. As they pass LYNN and VICKIE, FITZ holds out his hand to them.)

FITZ: Daughters of Jerusalem! Don't cry for me. You should be worrying about yourselves and your children. One of these days, terrible things are going to

happen here, and women will wish they didn't have any children.

(FITZ, MARIA, TROY, and ADRIAN walk slowly off STAGE RIGHT, but they return immediately.)

VICKIE (clapping her hands): Say, you boys were good! Wasn't that neat, Mrs. Sellards?

(All of them sit down again.)

MRS. SELLARDS: Yes, it was very good. That could have been an accurate portrayal of Simon's actions.

MARIA: This skit has given me a new insight into Simon's role in the crucifixion. I've always had the idea that he was forced to carry the cross and that he hated to do it. I prefer to think that he wanted to help Jesus.

TROY: Although the Bible doesn't tell us any more about Simon, I don't believe he carried the cross to Calvary and then forgot all about Jesus. He must have had some further interest in what happened.

MRS. SELLARDS: Let's continue our study along those lines. If you had been Simon, what else would you have done?

LYNN (shuddering): I'd have looked away when they were nailing Jesus to the cross. I don't believe I could have watched such a cruel thing.

VICKIE: Not me! I'd have stood beside Jesus to comfort him during his suffering. Maybe I could have wiped the blood off his face where the crown of thorns had broken the skin.

ADRIAN: And I'd have helped John take care of Mary. It would have been wonderful to have comforted the mother of Jesus when she was mourning for her son.

TROY: Maybe Simon helped Joseph carry Jesus to the tomb.

VICKIE: What do you suppose Simon did on the first day of the week when the news spread that Jesus was alive? After all, Simon had carried the cross, and perhaps he had watched Jesus die.

FITZ: In Simon's place, I would have raced with Peter and John to the garden to see for myself. But it would have been frightening to believe that someone had stolen his body.

TROY: I'll bet Simon stayed in Jerusalem until he knew for sure what had happened.

LYNN: And I'd like to think that Simon was at Bethany forty days later and heard Jesus say, "Go ye into all the world, and preach the gospel to every creature."

MARIA: He must have been influenced by what he had seen and heard. Just think, Simon may have been the first person to take the gospel to Africa.

ADRIAN: I'm sorry I made fun of your idea, Troy. This is the best program we've had for a long time.

VICKIE: I'll say! Simon of Cyrene won't be just a "name" to me anymore.

FITZ: That's right. I'll always think of Simon as the man who humbled himself to help Jesus.

MRS. SELLARDS: All of you have done very well in recreating Simon's story. Let us close our meeting with a silent prayer of thanksgiving for the death and resurrection of Jesus.

(They bow their heads.)   □

CURTAIN

A Meditation Around Death and Resurrection Events in Jesus' Life

● by Carolyn Jennings
and J. A. Morrison

The following meditation was used in place of a sermon at an Easter dawn service by the youth of the Brighton Community Church in Tonawanda, New York. Staging is simple and can be adapted to your own situation.

NARRATOR: It is after the Supper, and Jesus and some of his friends are walking when Judas and some officers approach Jesus. Jesus moves a bit ahead of his friends to approach Judas directly. Judas extends his hand to Jesus while the officers watch.

JUDAS *(with hesitation and obvious mental pain):* Friend . . . I . . .

JESUS: Judas, are you sure?

JUDAS: Jesus, you know I believe in you as a person—this is nothing against you personally—and I believe in much of what you are doing. But . . .

JESUS: Judas—are you sure?

JUDAS: Jesus—DON'T . . .

JESUS: Judas, you have been with me all these months. Why are you doing this?

JUDAS: What you are doing is wrong. You are upset-

J. A. Morrison is Pastor and Carolyn Jennings is a lay person at the Brighton Community Church of Tonawanda, New York.

ting the people, and you are not giving them the kind of leadership they want.

JESUS: I am telling them how they can make their lives count.

JUDAS *(turns to an officer):* It is no use. I can't talk with him anymore. He was my friend, but he is wrong. I want to press the charges.

NARRATOR: The officer reaches to take Jesus. Peter, we are told, has a great attack of bravery and lunges for the officer. Jesus stops Peter.

JESUS: Peter! Stop!

PETER: Assassin! Traitor!

JESUS: Peter! That is not *our* way. REMEMBER!

PETER: I'll remember. I'll remember for as long as I live—if I live.

JESUS: Peter—soon your bravery will be gone, but you must still remember. You will live. I will live. Not as I do now, but I *will* live. Remember. And one thing more—he is doing what seems right for him.

PETER: Right? What's *right?* How many times have we heard that throughout history?

JESUS: We must live as we have been teaching these past months. If we do not, neither our living nor our dying will make any difference.

NARRATOR: The officer leads Jesus away and Peter, subdued and turns in the opposite direction. Later, Peter finds his way to a gathering outside the place where the authorities are interrogating Jesus. A woman approaches Peter.

WOMAN: Are you Simon—I mean, Peter?

PETER: Why do you ask?

WOMAN: Don't you know Jesus?

PETER: Who?

WOMAN: Come now, Peter. You know who I mean!

PETER (somewhat softly and hesitantly): I—uh—knew him, once.

WOMAN: What do you mean—knew him? You know him now—you were with him.

PETER: NO! I DON'T! I only thought I did! (More anger than denial.)

WOMAN: Then you admit it! You could be implicated. You DO know him!

PETER: I know nothing. He is weak.

WOMAN: We all are.

PETER: But he could have been strong.

WOMAN: YOU could be strong.

PETER: I am!

WOMAN: I know—but not that way.

PETER: Then what way?

WOMAN: Do you know Jesus?

PETER: Leave me alone!

WOMAN: Peter—he's going to need you.

PETER: No one can help him now. He destroyed the only chance he had. Why? I ask myself—will I fail also?

NARRATOR: We are told then that a rooster began to crow, and it appears to us, from reading the account, that Peter got his answer. But it is now after the trial, and it is the day of the crucifixion. Mary Magdalene (MM) and Mary the Mother of Jesus (MJ) are hushed and hidden near the cross. Mary Magdalene begins to speak.

MM: If only . . .

MJ: Don't! . . . Quiet . . . please! They're nearly gone and they. . . .

MM (weeping): My God. . . . Why? How? Why—why . . .

MJ (in loud whisper): Mary—please be still! They'll hear. There is nothing more we can do. He will suffer no more!

MM: I wish I could hold him again. Love him again. Warm. Tender.

MJ: Yes. He was loving. Look, even now, after all the pain, he seems peaceful. LISTEN! What are the soldiers saying? Shhhhh.

MM: I cannot hear them. Can you hear what they are saying? (Pause.) What are they doing? (Louder.) Oh, no! (Realizes they are removing JESUS from the cross.) Please—NO!

MJ: QUIET! They will chase us away. We must stay close. Wait! Look! They are letting Joseph have him. Let's see where he takes him so that we can tell the others and anoint him. Maybe, even now, we can bring comfort.

NARRATOR: They did find the tomb, and they did carry out the message of hope and comfort. It is early Sunday, and Mary Magdalene has taken the chance of going to the grave to check on her friend one more time. Imagine Mary walking to the tomb thinking these thoughts.

MM: I cannot get over that awful sense of the sickening thud when they dropped him. Jesus—my friend, my loving, good friend. How much you gave us, taught us, showed us! But that thud! That three-foot drop into that hole. You, nailed to the cross—drop—thud! O my God! Do you remember, dear friend, how often you needed a tender delicate hand to reach to you, to massage your pain? Do you know, even now, how we gave and loved, how we held each other in hope? That in the midst of great pain, we loved, we laughed, we cried, we gathered, we separated, and when you needed it, we tried to keep you from . . . from heading straight into trouble. We stayed, we hoped, we gave—and now, as I come to your tomb, I sense something. . . . It's almost like you said—but it can't be! (Sees empty tomb.) No! Now they have . . . oh, no! . . . Peter! Peter! Where are you? They stole him. They killed him and now they stole him. Oh, Peter! Can't they leave us alone?

NARRATOR: I imagine that Mary wept quietly for a moment—maybe sobbed. Then, Jesus speaks to her.

JESUS: Mary! Mary, my friend.

MM: No. No more tricks, please.

JESUS (softly and tenderly): Mary!

MM: Teacher? Is it you? Really you?

NARRATOR: There is that moment when two people who have known each other so well look each other in the eye and for that beautiful moment know that the miracle has occurred. You have moments like that yourself. But let's look at what happened next. Mary is running to tell some of the others. Out of breath, she runs up to some of Jesus' friends.

MM (excited): I must tell you! Listen to me! I have seen Christ! He is alive! Mary and I talked with Him! Listen. . . .

NARRATOR: No one listens. No one believes.

MM (quietly, but emphatically—deliberately): I TELL YOU—I WAS WITH HIM. I SAW HIM; I TALKED WITH HIM. (Turning to Peter.) Please, Peter, I did see him and he wanted me to tell you, Peter. Jesus is alive! Maybe I am the first to say it, but I know it and I'll say it again, and again, and again. No one will stop me.

NARRATOR: Well, we know that Mary didn't stop. We know that she finally persuaded some others to take up the story. Have you ever thought how often people have had trouble believing good news and have wanted somehow to stop it? It is some time after the scene we just saw, and two of Jesus' friends are walking along one of the local roads. They are discussing the crucifixion and the events leading up to it.

FRIEND I: I simply can't understand this. Maybe we could have done something more. He did not need to die.

FRIEND II: I do not see what we could have done.

FRIEND I: But why must it always be that a good person has to go through all of that?

FRIEND II: That is the way life is. It seems you can't

ever count on things being the way you want them. Perhaps we were mistaken about Jesus.

FRIEND I: But we weren't. At least I don't think so. He did have some good things to say.

FRIEND II: He should have been stronger. You know some of his friends tried to tell him that he was getting into trouble.

NARRATOR: Jesus joins them. They do not recognize him. He speaks.

JESUS: Who got into trouble?

FRIEND I: Jesus of Nazareth. We had such hope in him, but they killed him.

FRIEND II (interrupting): But some women say they saw him, that he is alive. I wish I could believe that.

FRIEND I: Yes, but it is rather hard to believe.

JESUS: Why is it so difficult to believe? Don't seeds die and become flowers? Don't you end one part of your life and start another? Birth, for example. Or child to youth? Or youth to adult?

FRIEND I: But this isn't the same. It's different . . . more like a miracle that couldn't happen.

JESUS: Love always is a miracle.

NARRATOR: We are told that the three had dinner together, and as they were eating, Jesus took the bread and said the blessing and gave it to them.

The two friends look at Jesus and then at each other as the reality of who their companion is dawns on them. They speak.

FRIEND I or II (intermittently): My God. I never thought . . . but it is true. Jesus, it is really you.

Your words,
    Your actions,
        Your dreams,
            Your hopes,
                Your belief in each one of us.
                    Your desire for justice and peace.
                        Your great movement for God's
                            will to be done.

Alive! Now!   □

SYMBOLS OF THE RESURRECTION

In a day which seeks immediate practicality and the real thing, signs and symbols still play an important part in our thinking. Trademarks, traffic signs, type styles, logos, etc., all bring to mind an immediate identification and evoke feelings about the substance the symbol represents.

So it is with Easter. Even the name is a symbol—coming from the old Saxon word for the personification of the East, the morning, and spring: Ostara, Osterr, or Eastre. As such, the word is the symbol evoking feelings of joy, lightheartedness, and hope.

The use of symbols is hardly new with Christianity. Consider the significance of these Old Testament symbols: the sabbath, the rainbow, circumcision, Jacob's ladder, the many sacrifices, the priestly vestments, the Passover, the tabernacle and temple appointments, memorial rock piles, the names of Isaiah's sons, Jeremiah's and Ezekiel's use of ''visual aids,'' and others. Jesus also used symbols—particularly in his parables: the vine, the mustard seed, the lamp, the hen, and so forth.

A symbol, of course, is not an end in itself, but a guide to deeper meaning. To that end, we are including on the following pages a few symbols of Easter with a brief explanation of each.

You might use these as a beginning for class discussion on the resurrection and its meaning for Christians today—or simply as classroom decorations. If so, there are a number of ways to do this:

- Cut the symbols out and hold them up for all to see as you would a poster, commenting on their meaning.
- Make a mobile with the symbols.
- Ask students to enlarge the symbols into posters.
- Decorate a bulletin board or wall with the symbols.
- Ask students to think up their own symbol for Easter.
- Ask students to recall other symbols of Easter and to discuss what they mean (e.g., eggs, chickens and rabbits, the empty cross, the lamb with a flag, etc.).
- Trace these five symbols onto a ditto master and make take-home copies for children to color.

BUTTERFLY

The butterfly has long been a symbol of the resurrection—for obvious reasons. As the caterpillar encases itself willingly in its chrysalis (cocoon) and later emerges to a more beautiful body, so Christ willingly encased himself in the tomb and emerged to his glorified body.

Significantly, the flight of the butterfly represents not only the divine capabilities of the risen Christ but also the highest hopes of humanity for the joy and excitement of soaring freedom under the love of God. As such, both the butterfly and the resurrected Christ call men to faith and to their own life, death, and resurrection.

POMEGRANATE

In Greek and Latin mythology, the pomegranate was the sign of Prosphore/Proserpina, the goddess of spring and new life. Christians have used the plant, filled with seeds and ready to burst open, to symbolize Christ, ready to burst open the tomb and to give life to his believers.

Because of the countless seeds unified in the one fruit, the pomegranate has also come to symbolize the unity of Christians ready to break forth into new life with God, now and in eternity.

The symbol further suggests the fertility of the Word, which will bring forth fruit, and the richness of divine grace.

LILY

Although the lily abundantly decorates altars and homes on Easter, it didn't always. Adapted from pre-Christian symbolism, the lily was a symbol of purity, an attribute of the virgin saints, particularly the virgin Mary. In Renaissance art the lily is often shown at the annunciation—either in the hand of the archangel Gabriel, in Mary's hand, or in a vase beside her.

Perhaps because the lily blooms at Easter, perhaps because of its trumpet shape, perhaps because of the fleur-de-lis' association with royalty, the lily today symbolizes the heralding of new life for believers in the resurrected King. Although its bulb is buried in the ground, new life springs forth at Easter.

PHOENIX

The phoenix, alleges Egyptian mythology, is a beautiful bird which lives in the Arabian desert for five hundred years. Then, having fulfilled its life, it bursts into flames and is destroyed—only to rise again from its own ashes. Unlike caterpillars, which are transformed, the phoenix is totally destroyed—yet is resurrected. In addition to symbolizing the resurrection event, the mythological "fact" that there is only one such bird fits well with our need for only one resurrected Savior.

Clement, one of the first Christian writers after the apostles (c. A.D. 100), was the first to connect the phoenix with the resurrection of Jesus.

PEACOCK

An ancient legend has it that the peacock sheds its feathers only to grow others more brilliant than those it has lost. Another legend says that the flesh of the peacock does not decay.

It is easy to see why this bird became an early symbol of the resurrection. As the peacock's flesh does not decay, so the flesh of Christ did not see corruption in the grave. Rather, he returned in a glorified body, more brilliant than the one he shed on the cross.

An Easter Calendar

● by Sally E. Stuart

Easter should be one of the most exciting events of the year in our church school classes, but often it rushes by with scarcely more than a simple recalling of the story of Jesus' death and resurrection. Since this is not only the basis of our gospel, but also a highly complex and intriguing story, we need to work at bringing it to life for our students.

The older your students are, the more background information you will need to make available to the students. For young children it will be sufficient to help them understand the events and their sequence by having them draw or glue pictures on a wall mural after studying the story. They could also act out portions. As simply and directly as possible, answer the questions they ask.

School-age children, and even youth or adults, will benefit from a more in-depth study of the events and related background. For older children's classes you may need to do the initial research by gathering appropriate books.

The children might use their newfound knowledge to create shoebox dioramas or tabletop scenes depicting the various events of Easter week. Stimulate interest by asking questions that will prick their curiosity. On what day of the week was Jesus arrested? How big was the stone that sealed the tomb? What were the burial customs of the day? The reference books, which you gather into your classroom from the church or public library, should contain the answers to the questions that you ask and to other questions that your students are likely to ask. If it is important to save time, you may want to mark the location of the answers for them to find. However, the more the students are involved, the more they will learn.

It may be helpful to clarify the sequence of events during Jesus' last week by using a time chart, calendar, or other visual aid. Finding this information can be included in the research assignments, but it will go roughly like this: Palm Sunday—Triumphal entry into Jerusalem and teaching in the temple. Monday—Chasing money-changers from the temple. Tuesday—Jesus went to the temple for the last time, ending his public ministry. Wednesday—Judas made plans to betray Jesus; Jesus was probably in or near Bethany. Thursday—The Lord's Supper; Jesus prayed in the Garden of Gethsemane and was arrested. Friday—Jesus was taken before Annas and Caiaphas about 1 A.M., before the Sanhedrin before daylight, and to Pilate about dawn; he went before Herod, returned to Pilate, and was sentenced and then crucified; he died about 3 P.M. and was buried before sundown. Saturday—It was the Jewish sabbath; Roman guards watched the tomb. Sunday—Jesus arose!

After the research is completed and all of their questions are answered, let the class members decide which events they will transform into dioramas or tabletop scenes. Depending on the size of the class, the students can work individually or in groups of two or more. Keep everyone involved. The older the children are, the more detailed their scenes will be. Supply construction paper, chenille sticks, twigs, moss, stones, papier-mâché, clay, poster paint, and other supplies as needed to complete the scenes.

Older children might enjoy creating a "Time Line of Easter Week" to display in a hallway or the narthex for the entire church to study. It should reveal as much of their research as possible. Children might also write up each event of the week as a news story and print it in a "Bethany Bugle," or "Jerusalem Journal." Their newspaper could be distributed to the congregation or even to neighborhood homes along with invitations to attend Easter services.

Extend your Easter celebration this year and have fun! □

Easter Traditions and the Child's Response

● by Kathy Gehris

A tradition is the passing down from generation to generation of ideas, customs, beliefs, and stories. In preparation for the coming of Easter, we as Sunday church school teachers become aware of the many traditions of this season in the church.

On Palm Sunday we remember Jesus' triumphal entry into Jerusalem and the rejoicing of the people as they laid down their garments and palm branches in his path. The palms and stories enable us and our children to catch

Kathy Gehris is a free-lance writer and Christian educator living in Shermansdale, Pennsylvania.

some of the spirit of commitment and embarkation on a chosen path.

Maundy Thursday becomes our mandate of love for one another in Christ. We may wash one another's feet and share Communion together in renewal of our oneness with our Lord.

Good Friday solemnly recalls Jesus' passion and death, stirring in us mourning and penitence. We may participate in services representing the seven stations of the cross.

And then on Easter morning there is a watch at dawn,

anticipation of a new rising of the sun and greetings of "He is risen!" with "He is risen indeed!" To some of us the sun truly dances in celebration, while to others it effectively overcomes the darkness once again and brings to light all the earth's new life.

Children may hunt for eggs, which are yet another symbol of new life and resurrection.

Church bells ring. People gather for worship, some in new clothes—another symbol of new life—many wearing or carrying flowers, all with a sense of joy and excitement. People who rarely if ever come to church are drawn to the congregation of believers on Easter.

As adults in the church, we remember the Easters of our childhood, the history of the traditions of the church, the teachings of Jesus, the meaning it all has to our lives and our faith. How, then, do children respond to these traditions in the church?

Highly symbolic words are beyond the understanding of elementary children. They relate their thinking to what they see and know from their own experience. They do not see hidden meanings or find parallels to stories, songs, or dramatizatons.

When six-year-old Jessica goes to the sunrise service with her parents, she expects to see the sun rise. She makes no connection with the Son or the resurrection. She sees people she loves and trusts come together to watch the sun come over the horizon; she senses the joy and excitement, and she also feels happy.

When four-year-old Ellie finds (with considerable help from family and friends) a colored egg in the grass, she knows that she found a beautiful surprise, that others are finding surprises, too, and that it is a happy day! She does not know the egg is a symbol of new life and a way to remind us of Jesus' message of the resurrection.

On Easter morning when ten-year-old Eliud stands with his four sisters and his mother and father singing, "Christ the Lord is risen today, Alleluia!" he may not understand fully what the words mean. But he sees his Sunday church school teacher, his Uncle Tony, his church family, and even the policeman on the corner all joyfully singing together, and he senses the spirit we call renewal.

The inclusion of children in the traditions of the church at Easter gives them a sense of belonging to the church family now. They feel secure in their place in God's creation, and some even acknowledge their part in the ongoingness of this creation.

Symbolism may or may not be grasped, but we as teachers trust in the concrete learnings of today as foundations for the connections that can be made at a later period of readiness in each child's maturing life.

Jeffrey's appreciation for the lovely flower that grows out of the dry, brown tulip bulb is just that at nine years old, but at twenty-nine he might better make the jump of faith from the flower to death as we know it and to resurrection.

Our role as Sunday church school teachers is one of inclusion, provision, and appreciation. As we include children in the traditional celebration of Easter, we open the door to their belonging and their sense of history in the church. "Oh, look, there are those lily flowers again—just like last year!"

When families attend Communion services on Maundy Thursday, children sense the ritual and the sharing. Then again at Grandma's house on Sunday they share in another communion, a joyful gathering of loved ones, just like last year; and not now, but some day or year, just like Jesus and the disciples.

We can provide experiences for our church school children that enable them to relate to meaningful celebration. Through role play older elementary children can integrate fact with feeling and find points of identification with biblical stories and understandings. When children's experiences are explored and then biblical stories and traditions are experienced, there is more likelihood of their comprehending.

In many areas of the country nature provides us with so many visible signs of new life . . . flowers, budding trees, baby animals. This rhythm of nature is a concrete awareness for child and adult together of the regular renewal of life in all forms.

Whenever we relate to children, whether including them in whole church experiences or providing experiential learning situations, natural questions and observations surface. We appreciate these opportunities for shared teaching/learning. When we have taken time to stay centered in our relationship with God and seek the direction we need in our lives and in our preparation for our time with the children, we feel more comfortable with the spontaneous questions that come forth and our ability to search for the answers together.

It's helpful to remember to try to answer questions honestly and openly and simply to answer the questions asked. We appreciate also new learnings from the imaginative understandings of children when we fully listen to the spirit of our shared explorations and learnings.

Easter calls forth a response from adult and child, and we in love share those responses through our traditions and understandings of them. "Christ the Lord is risen today. Alleluia!"	□

Try to Remember

A one-act play for the Lenten season

• by Bradford H. Lyle

Cast of Characters
Mother Henderson
Jim Henderson
Amy Henderson
Jan and Sissy Henderson
Carl Henderson
Mr. Swenson

SCENE 1

The setting is the front room of a small farmhouse forty-five years ago. The room has a table and four chairs in the foreground. To the left is a fireplace and rocking chair. MOTHER HENDERSON is seated in the rocker and is quietly humming to herself. Her children, JIM, AMY, JAN, and SISSY appear, walking toward the door.

AMY: Mom . . . we'll be back by ten.
MOTHER: Now wait just a minute . . . you're not going out on the eve of Ash Wednesday . . .
JAN *(in a pleading voice):* Oh, Mother! *(Looks at others.)*
JIM: Peter and Frank are waiting for me at Pop's Drug Store . . .
AMY: And I told Sue I'd be over tonight . . .
SISSY: Jan and I wanted to ride our bikes over to Heinrich's . . .
MOTHER *(with firmness, shaking her head):* Ever since your father died, we go through this; you remember what he asked of you each year at this time—heaven knows it's little enough! You remember that he asked you to spend this one evening every year studying the Scriptures like he

The author is Pastor of the East Dover Baptist Church, Toms River, New Jersey.

used to do. And I shouldn't have to remind the four of you every year, now should I?
JIM *(resigned to studying, but with understanding):* No, Mom, you shouldn't. Come on, Jan, . . . Amy, . . . Sis. . . . I'll get the Bible; you get around the fireplace with Mom. *(Goes to get the Bible while others gather around MOTHER HENDERSON. JIM returns with Bible, pausing, looking at his mother, and sits down.)*
MOTHER: I remember how your father used to talk to us about the meaning of Lent at this time every year, around this same fireplace. Remember Janny?
JAN: Yes . . . I remember he used to say it had something to do with what Jesus went through for us . . .
JIM *(with impatience):* Where would you like me to begin reading, Mom?
MOTHER: Oh, begin where Jesus tells the disciples he has to go to Jerusalem, if you would please, Jimmy.
(JIM looks up Matthew 16:21-26, reads slowly, then puts Bible down and stares into space.)
AMY *(with concern):* What's the matter, Jim?
JIM *(some anger in his voice):* Nothing that some time with the guys won't cure—I'm leaving, Mom. *(Starts to get up; MOTHER takes his arm.)*
MOTHER: Jimmy. . . .
JIM *(explosive and bitter):* Oh, Mom! "Suffer many things . . . take up the cross . . . lose your life" . . . all the things Dad did . . . and what did it get him? An early grave! Dad was a real Christian—gave anyone the shirt off his back for the asking . . . and what did he ever get out of it? What did we ever get?
MOTHER: James Henderson!

JIM: It's the truth, Mom, and we might as well face it! *(Runs to door, exits.)*

SISSY *(goes to comfort MOTHER, gently):* Mom, don't feel bad. He'll be back.

MOTHER *(shaking head, with heaviness):* No . . . I wonder if Jimmy will ever really come back. Ever since Daddy died, he's been so—so angry about things.

JAN: Don't worry; Jim will come back. *(Lights dim; all exit.)*

SCENE 2

After midnight. Same room with table in center. JIM silently enters, looks around, and slowly goes over to table, starts to reach for the Bible on table, and sits down in one of the chairs.

JIM *(with hesitation and frustration):* It sure doesn't make any sense to me. . . . *(Slowly lowers head on arms and falls asleep.)*

(Lights dim and JIM exits, to take part in some of the following sequences. The lights are then raised on four different "dream scenes," each taking place in the same room. In Dream Sequence I CARL HENDERSON, the father, enters the room, about to leave the house with box under arm; he is followed by MOTHER HENDERSON.)

MOTHER *(taking his arm):* Oh, Carl. Do you have to go out on a night like this? Couldn't the Smiths wait till morning?

MR. HENDERSON *(gently):* Now, Ellie, that young colt can't wait to be born! Guess this is what comes of knowing a little about animal doctoring. *(Chuckles to himself and puts arm around MRS. HENDERSON.)* I'll be back soon; keep the kettle on and don't worry. *(Exits, leaving MOTHER standing. Lights fade.)*

(Dream Sequence II: Lights raised on MOTHER, AMY, JAN, SISSY, and JIM around the table with birthday cake: all but JAN and SISSY are singing; the two girls look on with smiles.)

MOTHER, AMY, and JIM: Happy birthday to you, happy birthday, dear Jan and Sissy, happy birthday to you. *(Laughter; MR. HENDERSON enters.)*

MOTHER *(in a concerned voice):* Where have you been, Carl?

MR. HENDERSON *(troubled):* Got to go right out again; the Klan's been stirring up trouble at the Dickson farm . . . say they aim to run off Jesse Fallin . . . I'm going over to stay with them for a while.

MOTHER *(surprised, angry):* The Dickson farm? Carl Henderson, you owe those people nothing! They tried to buy us out three years ago when we were down on our luck!

MR. HENDERSON *(firm and quick):* That's all past and gone; John would do as much for me now; we've been through a lot together.

MOTHER *(excited now):* And what about the twins' birthdays? Will you just walk out on them, too?

MR. HENDERSON *(looks sadly at the twins, goes over, puts hands on their shoulders):* I'm sorry . . . you know how much I wanted us all to be together, especially tonight, but . . . well, the Dicksons are having trouble, and I think I need to be with them. Will you save me a big piece of that cake? *(JAN and SISSY nod yes.)*

MR. HENDERSON: Good! I'll be back as quickly as I can! Bye, Mother. *(Exits.)*

MOTHER: Children, you've got a good father, even if he is a little soft in the heart. *(Smiles, shakes head, lights dim.)*

(Dream Sequence III: MR. HENDERSON is sitting at the table, reading from the Bible. JIM comes over.)

JIM: Hi, Dad.

MR. HENDERSON: Oh, hello, Jimmy! *(With surprise, but pleased; pauses, looking closely at JIM.)* Looks like something might be on your mind.

JIM *(hesitating):* Dad . . . why do you read the Scriptures so much? I mean, Pete's dad and Frank's dad never read it, and they seem to be doing okay; why do you spend so much time on it?

MR. HENDERSON *(pauses, thinking):* Well, son . . . I wouldn't say it's a matter of doing all right— guess you can see by looking around our place that knowing about Jesus hasn't put us on Easy Street. *(Chuckling.)* No, Jim. It's something different . . . something hard to explain—a new way of looking at life, myself, and others; a love and a faith in something, in someone bigger than you or me or anyone; all I know is, I couldn't do without it. *(Pauses.)* I've found a friend—a real friend, Jimmy. I hope you find him, too. Now, how about checking that fence with me?

JIM *(excited and pleased):* Sure, Dad. *(Both exit; lights dim.)*

(Dream Sequence IV: MOTHER, JIM, JAN, AMY, and SISSY enter room; MOTHER is crying; the children try to comfort her.)

MOTHER: Oh, Carl . . . Carl . . .

JIM *(holding MOTHER'S arm):* Mom, it's going to be all right . . . *(Knock at door; AMY answers. MR. SWENSON enters, goes over to MOTHER.)*

MR SWENSON: We're sure sorry, Ellie; Carl was a wonderful man. We'll never forget his kindness; the winter you folks supplied us with food and paid for Ingrid's medicine; and not asking for a thing in return. This old world needs more like him, I can tell you.

(Lights dim, then are raised on JIM, still sleeping at table. AMY enters, seeing JIM.)

AMY *(excited):* Mother! Jan! Sissy! Jim's home! He did come back, just like Jan said! *(JIM awakes, rubs eyes, looking around him; MOTHER HENDERSON gives him a hug.)*

MOTHER *(relieved):* Oh, Jimmy . . . I was so worried!

JIM *(trying to reassure; carefully choosing words):* No need to worry; I just took a walk and came back, guess I fell asleep. I feel different this morning— better somehow. Mom, I know now why Dad did the things he did. He was quite a man, wasn't he?

MOTHER: Yes, Jimmy . . . quite a man. Now, how about some breakfast? *(Lights dim.)* □

Christian News Update: Did You Know Jesus?

● by Stanley White

Cast of Characters

PETER
MARY, MOTHER OF JESUS
PILATE
SOLDIER
MARY OF BETHANY
JOSEPH
NICODEMUS
REPORTER ON THE SCENE
BARABBAS
ANCHOR PERSON

ANCHOR PERSON: Good afternoon and welcome to Christian News Update. Today we are going back into time to the crucifixion of Christ. Now let's tune in with our on-the-scene news reporter, __(name)__.

REPORTER: Hello, I'm here with Peter, one of Christ's beloved disciples. Peter, when did you first come in contact with Jesus Christ?

PETER (sobbing): I was a fisherman along with my brother, Andrew, when I first met him. He called me Peter, meaning rock. I didn't clearly understand what he was talking about when he said he would depart from us. (Cries out painfully.) I boasted that I would lay down my life for him. When they arrested my Lord, my brother and I followed the crowd to the high priest's palace. I went to the yard where the fire was and there I denied him three times before the cock crowed. Just like he said I would—three times, man, three! It was the darkest hour of my life.

REPORTER: A man who was anointed by God, one whom you loved dearly and said you would lay down your life for—why?

PETER: I was so afraid they might suspect me; I was scared. I cannot talk anymore. I . . . I can't talk. . .

REPORTER: But . . . but . . . one more question . . .

PETER: No more . . . (Runs off.)

REPORTER: Pardon me, Miss, did you know Jesus? What is your name?

MARY OF
BETHANY: My name is Mary. I come from Bethany. Jesus was a frequent guest at my family's home. He last came to my home after my brother, Lazarus, had died. (Sobs.) I told him if he had come earlier, my brother would not have died. I questioned him as to why he didn't come sooner.

REPORTER: What was his reply? What was his mood in replying? Was he angry?

MARY OF
BETHANY: No, he didn't rebuke me for my statement. I learned that he had said that Lazarus was only sleeping and that he also had said he was the resurrection.

REPORTER: What do you mean, Mary? What happened? What did Jesus do?

MARY OF
BETHANY: He told me to roll the stone from the door of the tomb. Then he called out to Lazarus. Lazarus came forth—I mean Lazarus got up out of the tomb and came to him. He had raised him from the dead! He had made him come to life again! He was so good to us. I . . . I can't believe this has happened to him. Once he said he would not always be with us. (Sobbing.) I never thought it would end this way.

REPORTER: Thank you, Miss.

(MARY walks off sobbing.)

REPORTER: Sir . . . sir . . . can I speak with you?

PILATE: Why? . . . What about? . . . Pertaining to whom?

REPORTER: Jesus, sir; did you know him?

PILATE: No! . . . I have nothing to say on the subject of that man.

REPORTER: But, sir, the world is watching and waiting for your views on Jesus. Please just let me talk to you for a minute.

PILATE: Oh! . . . (Stepping back.)

REPORTER: Didn't you condemn him to death, to die on the cross?

PILATE: Hold on. No! . . . Not at all. The Jews condemned him. It was not my choice. I washed my

The author is a student in the senior high class of the church school of the Calvary Baptist Church, Vaux Hall, New Jersey.

hands of it. Jews . . . his own people crucified him, not I or Rome. I wanted Barabbas to go to the cross, not this dreamer or so-called god.

REPORTER: But he was the Son of God. The Messiah.

PILATE: I have my own gods—Zeus, Apollo, Mercury, and Caesar. I do not wish to talk of the dreamer.

REPORTER: All right, you have your views; but just one more question.

PILATE: All right, one more question.

REPORTER: If you as governor of Judea had the power, why didn't you have him released?

PILATE: Because several problems arose with these Jews, and I was under a lot of pressure from the Jews. As I said earlier, it was their choice. (PILATE walks proudly away.)

REPORTER: Pardon me, sir, who are you? What is your relationship to Jesus?

BARABBAS: My name is Barabbas. I stand for freedom for my brothers in the Roman prisons. (Acts tough.)

REPORTER: What is your relationship to Christ who was crucified?

BARABBAS: I didn't know the man. I am a rebel, rebelling against the Roman rule of Judea. I hate their taxes and the way they treat our people.

REPORTER: Oh! Oh! . . . Thank you, sir; I understand your cause.

(BARABBAS storms off.)

REPORTER: Sir, may I have a few words with you? I can see you are very upset about what has happened to Jesus. Could you just tell me if you knew him. Oh, I'm sorry—what is your name?

NICODEMUS: My name is Nicodemus. I am a Pharisee and a member of the Jewish court in Jerusalem. I first saw him when he came to the Passover feast in Jerusalem. I met him that night. I acknowledged him as a teacher sent by God. I didn't understand all that he said to me at first. (Sobs deeply.)

REPORTER: What didn't you understand?

NICODEMUS: I didn't understand what he meant by being born again to see the Lord's kingdom.

REPORTER: You mean born out of the womb of your mother?

NICODEMUS: That is what I thought at first, my friend. *(Smiling through his tears.)* No, Jesus told me I must be born again by water and the Spirit. My rebirth is not of the body, but of the Holy Spirit. *(Sobbing.)*

REPORTER: It's all right. *(Patting NICODEMUS on the shoulder.)*

NICODEMUS: I . . . I . . . I tried to help him, I did. I spoke in his behalf at the trial. They wouldn't listen; they didn't understand the good he stood for. I had heard of how he made the blind to see and the crippled to walk. *(Sobbing.)*

REPORTER: I understand, sir. Thank you.

(NICODEMUS walks away with his head down.)

REPORTER: Soldier, sir, may I have a word with you, please?

SOLDIER: Yes! . . . What is it?

REPORTER: Were you at the crucifixion today? . . . What did you know of Christ?

SOLDIER: Well, I knew him not, but I was there. My friends gambled for his sandals and robe at the foot of the cross. Like the fools they are. I felt sorry for him. He didn't look like the type of person who would cause trouble.

REPORTER: What type of look did he have?

SOLDIER: Gentle—his eyes, his face—I can't explain it. Oh, yes, I remember just before he died, he called for Elijah. He then said that he was thirsty; so I gave him some wine on a sponge; he turned away. After three hours of darkness, Jesus cried out.

REPORTER: What did he cry out? Tell me. The world must know.

SOLDIER: He cried out in triumph: "It is finished. Father, into thy hands I commend my spirit." Then he died. When I saw that, I said, "Surely this was a righteous man." He was the Son of God . . . oh, and after that, one of the centurions pierced his side with his spear, and water came out. After seeing all this, I am sure this was the Son of God. We hung him between two thieves like a criminal! What have we done? . . . We killed him. . . . I don't want to speak about this innocent man anymore.

REPORTER: Well, we are running short of time, but I think we have time for one more interview . . . before we return to the News Center. . . . Miss, may I have a word with you about Jesus? I can see you are very upset, but, please, just one minute. That is all.

MARY: I am Mary, the mother of Jesus. *(Holds back a sob.)*

REPORTER: Well, folks, this is it, the one you have waited for: Christ's mother. How did you know you were being chosen by God to give birth to the Messiah?

MARY: Well, I knew because an angel came to me, the angel Gabriel. No one believed me then; so I traveled with my husband, Joseph, of Nazareth, to pay taxes in Bethlehem. When we got there, there were great crowds of people and the inn was full. We had to stay in a stable with the animals. But God made a way for us—this was the place where I gave birth to Jesus. Shepherds were led there after an angel had appeared to them as they watched over their sheep. . . . Wise men came to the house to see the baby Jesus. We went to Egypt because we were warned that Herod was looking for Jesus.

REPORTER: Why did you say you went to Egypt?

MARY: Herod sought to kill every boy two years old and under in Bethlehem so that he would be sure Jesus was among them. He was afraid Jesus would grow up and steal his kingdom, that Jesus was the King of the Jews.

REPORTER: Jesus has been reported to be the Son of God. Did he show signs of this in his early childhood?

MARY: Why, yes. Every year Joseph and I would go to Jerusalem for the feast of the Passover. When Jesus was twelve years old, he stayed behind. We looked for him for three days among the other children along the way home. When we couldn't find him, we went back to Jerusalem.

REPORTER: Where was he?

MARY: He was in the temple, listening and asking questions. I was upset and asked him why he had done this. He replied, "I was about my Father's work." Until he was thirty Jesus lived and worked as a carpenter. He grew in wisdom as well as stature. I saw him, as the Son of God, perform his first miracle.

REPORTER: What did he do?

MARY: He turned water into wine at a wedding in Galilee. When he left home, he traveled into the wilderness where he was baptized by John the Baptist. A voice from heaven said, as a dove descended upon his shoulders, "This is my beloved Son, in whom I am well pleased." Then Jesus had a great following of people wherever he went; people came from near and far to hear him preach and perform miracles. Of course, it breaks my heart and saddens me to see my son, who was so good, go from the cradle to the cross like a thief. But he was born for this hour. *(She wipes the tears from her eyes.)* He was the Son of God. But you wait and see; he will rise again from the grave. He will come again. *(Breaks down and cries.)* In three days we shall see him again; this is not the end.

(JOSEPH runs over to MARY.)

JOSEPH: Come, Mary. *(They turn and walk away.)*

REPORTER: Well, I guess that wraps it up. You have heard it from the people who were there at the scene of the crucifixion. But this crucifixion is not the end because the body of Christ is not in the tomb. Because we know from the Bible that the grave couldn't hold him. He rose on the third day, and he lives within the hearts of all of us who love him and believe on his name. He has not left us alone. This is ___(name) signing off from the scene at Calvary. Back to our News Center.

This play took place immediately following a morning worship service, and many of the members were able to witness this program who normally would not have returned for the program if scheduled for an earlier or later time.

The students who participated ranged in age from nine to seventeen.

□

Easter Interview

• **by Bradford Lyle**

(The backdrop is that of the Palestine countryside. The interviewer-commentator for local station J.E.R.U. appears.)

COMMENTATOR: Good morning, folks; Casey, the commentator, here with your worldwide news roundup. Well, this is the place all right; this is where the brief career of that most controversial young preacher from Nazareth finally came to an end just two short days ago. We tried to keep you up to date on his teaching, his healing, his harsh attacks on the government and religious leaders. You saw first-hand his entry just last week into Jerusalem. What an exciting time that was! Then, it seemed the luck of this young whirlwind ran out. He began losing his popular appeal—I'm told even his closest friends left his side at the end. And who could soon forget that grim scene of his death? Yes, this is where it all ended. Ah!. . . here comes two of his. . . followers, I suppose. Let's see if we can get a word from them. *(Enter MARY MAGDALENE and the other MARY.)* Remember, folks, you saw it right here on J.E.R.U.! Excuse me, ladies . . . I realize this is a sad time, but could you tell us a little about your departed leader?

MARY MAGDALENE: He was such a good man . . .

MARY: Yes . . . so kind and courageous . . .

COMMENTATOR: It's a shame what happened; it seems the good do die young. Looks like something's been going on this morning, too. *(Turns in direction of tomb.)* I noticed the entrance stone has been moved—

MARY MAGDALENE: The tomb! Oh, Mary, let's hope they haven't done anything more to our teacher and friend.

The author is Pastor of the East Dover Baptist Church, Toms River, New Jersey.

MARY: Yes . . . haven't they done enough? Can't they leave him in peace? Let's go see, Magdalene. *(They exit toward tomb.)*

COMMENTATOR: Well, folks, we'll soon know just what's been going on here. We'll have all the pertinent facts, information, and news analysis from our exclusive interview with these two fine ladies. *(The two Marys come running back.)* Ah! Here they come now. Well, ladies, what word from the tomb?

MAGDALENE *(excitedly):* Jesus lives! Oh, Jesus Christ is risen as promised!

MARY: Praise God! We must run to tell the others! *(Both pass by.)*

COMMENTATOR: Ladies! Wait! He did . . . what? . . . Stay tuned, folks; we'll have this temporary difficulty straightened out immediately. Don't turn your dial yet. *(PETER and JOHN now appear, running.)* Whoa, fellows; I'd like a brief word with you. I take it you were also his followers. Could you *please* tell this reporter what is going on?

JOHN: Two of the women who also were followers with us have just come to us saying that our Lord is no longer in the tomb, that he is risen! We wanted to see for ourselves.

PETER: It's very important that I know if this is true; you see, I denied and deserted him; and if he still lives, as he promised, I need his forgiveness.

JOHN: *All* of us need it, Peter; all of us left him when he most needed us. Come, let's hurry. *(They exit.)*

COMMENTATOR: Well, folks, this is a big news break for us! Women tend to get emotional, but now we have two level-headed men on the scene. Why, I'm sure that in just a few moments we'll have a reasonable explanation for you . . . *(PETER and JOHN come running back.)* . . . and here they are, just like I said! Now, men, could you tell in your own words for the people out there just what you saw and heard? Speak right into the mike.

PETER *(happily excited):* Jesus *does* live . . . and I know I am forgiven!

JOHN: Yes, praise God; our Lord lives! *(Both exit shouting, "Hallelujah!")*

COMMENTATOR *(puzzled, quieter):* Folks, I don't know what to tell you. I'm as confused as you. Our memorial service for a popular folk hero has turned into . . . I don't know what! Please bear with us; we'll get to the bottom of this somehow. Oh! Here comes a man who has the clear, cool look of a realist who can't be fooled. Excuse me, sir, could you tell us your name and what brings you here?

THOMAS: Thomas . . . my name is Thomas, if you must know, and I don't believe them . . . not a word of it, until I actually see the wounds in his hands and side, and touch them! Not until then will I say this is anything more than wishful thinking! *(Exits.)*

COMMENTATOR: You heard him, folks, and I know this one won't be easily taken in. Let's wait to hear his analysis. Hmmm . . . might be a good idea to do a special on him later this year. *(THOMAS returns, shaking his head.)* Ah, our man of the hour! Well, Thomas, let's get right down to the facts of this matter. What's your conclusion? Mass hypnosis? Power of suggestion? Hallucination?

THOMAS: My Lord and my God . . . my Lord and my God . . . he let me touch him . . . *(Walks off, as if in a happy daze.)*

COMMENTATOR: Eh? Thomas, wait! You can't . . . oh, well . . . there goes my special. What'll I do now? Oh, what's the use. Carl, stop shooting. Let's go home, gang; this one's beyond me! *(JESUS appears. COMMENTATOR notices him.)* Sorry, bud, the program's over . . . I've had it with covering this story. What? Still here? OK, OK; you might as well speak your piece . . . everyone else has!

JESUS: I stand at the door and knock . . . your door. If any open to me, I will enter their lives and be with them to give my peace, my life. This is my promise. You are troubled about many things. When you call, I will come. *(Exits.)*

COMMENTATOR: Wait! Gone . . . but I've got the feeling he's not really gone. Folks, I've got a reporter's hunch that for me, this story's only begun! ☐

Ceremony of Innocence

● by Mark Heydon

CHARACTERS

NARRATOR
CAIAPHAS
PILATE
BARABBAS
PETER
JUDAS
MARY, MOTHER OF JESUS
MARY MAGDALENE
(non-speaking:)
MIME (Spirit of Crowd)
JESUS
GUARD

STORY

The *Ceremony of Innocence* is the narrator's imagined story of Jesus Christ's trial, a trial where the accused stands passive for perhaps the first time and watches, with some disappointment, a stumbling and confused humanity try to regain control of itself through childish patter. Initially, a young childlike mime supplies visual expression for the hidden narrator's words, but, once the drama has started, the attention of the crowd is pulled away from the mime and, until the final speech, is concentrated on the actions and words of the innocents.

STAGING

There are no sets or props for the play besides the natural setting of a church's sanctuary. The play's historical setting is deliberately vague to allow a past, yet present, feeling. Consequently the characters are cas-

The author, a member of the First Chinese Baptist Church, California, is a teacher of English at the college level.

ually, but uniformly, dressed in modern clothes. Only Christ varies from the others in his dress, but just slightly with a plaid or brighter colored shirt. Most importantly, the audience is part of the play—it is the crowd and one of the innocents. Speeches, questions, and discussions are all directed towards the audience as actual participants in the play.

(MIME lies asleep at center stage. Slowly, as the NARRATOR reaches end of introduction, MIME stretches awake, gathers self up to observe approaching characters. MIME parodies characters as they enter.)

NARRATOR *(from periphery of sanctuary or auditorium):* This is the story—an old one and maybe a little tarnished from lack of recent use. It's the story of a man, a very young man by our standards, who appeared on this earth some two thousand years ago. It's also the story of the few men and women who were lucky enough to get to know him. But most importantly, it's the story of a god, our God, a God who, thousands of years ago, became a living creation and experienced life as a human. Now this experience is interesting because of what God in Jesus found. What God in Jesus eventually suffered here most was not the ridicule and anger of a bunch of long-ago, old men. What he found was the jealous abuse and cowardice of all humanity—past, present, and future. What follows now should sound pretty familiar. It's the doubts and fears and troubles we feel today. So, listen closely. Listen for your voice among the crowd, and, well, I see some of them coming now. Let me introduce you.

This first one is Caiaphas—leader, president, and conniving spokesperson for the Sanhedrin, the rulers

of the Jewish religious community. A special man—cunning enough to outwit the Roman governors, including Pilate, at every turn. Yet now he finds himself confronted with a new problem, a cheeky village rabbi called Jesus who is threatening his authority—not to mention his bank account.

CAIAPHAS (enters confidently from back of auditorium and struts to front): We must rid ourselves of this troublemaker. This man, Jesus, is getting too popular. He's stirring up the people with his radical teachings and magician's tricks. He's questioning our authority and the very laws that have kept us as the chosen people. That scoundrel overstepped himself for certain when he started that riot outside the temple, chasing our money changers and shoppers away from—what did he say?—"My Father's temple!" Blasphemy! Blasphemy! A lot of money was lost that day because of him. He'll pay for that. He's played himself right into our hands. I have set the wheel in motion that will crush him and rid us of him forever. (Pause.) And that idiot Pilate, whom the Romans sent to govern us, is going to help us! Son of God indeed! We shall see. (Sits front left in the audience.)

NARRATOR: And Pilate—seems destined always to be just two steps behind Caiaphas. Roman governor of Judea, Samaria, and Idumea, he's a military man who understands the power of the sword—or so he'd like to think—but in the case of this Jewish fellow, Jesus, he's found himself in over his head.

PILATE (enters from back to the front with military bearing): I haven't got time for this. These are Jewish troubles. Take care of them yourselves. I'll have none of it. Who put you up to this, anyway? I'll bet it was that character Caiaphas. Well, alright. But I answer to Rome, not to you. We'll give the man a fair hearing and be through with him, Caiaphas, and the lot of you. (Sits at right in the audience.)

NARRATOR: There's Barabbas. He's the option, another criminal, but—

BARABBAS (enters from back and crosses to front): There's no choice here, no choice at all. What've I done? I've fought to get the Romans off our backs. But this fraud's fighting everybody. He's worthless, I tell you. A bigmouth buffoon. (Sits short distance from Pilate.)

NARRATOR: There, that one's Peter, one of the disciples. Jesus said that Peter would deny him three times before the evening rooster crowed. Three times he would back down. And sure enough he denied Jesus three times. Today he doubts. He's wondering what exactly is going on.

PETER (timidly enters from back, crosses behind audience to auditorium right, behind and a distance away from Pilate): What are they doing? What are they talking about? They don't understand. I mean, they can't—ah, well, I—I'll sit over here and—

NARRATOR: And Judas here, another disciple. Notice his walk. He's worried. Things haven't gone according to plan—his plan—but he hasn't given up. He's got a hero, the kind of hero dreams are made of.

JUDAS (enters anxiously from back, crosses behind audience and to auditorium left, behind and a distance away from Caiaphas): He's up on charges, but—but he can perform miracles, big, show-off miracles that will prove what a fantastic person he is! (And that'll show just what a fantastic person I, Judas, am.) The bigger the miracle, the better. He's going to show them.

NARRATOR: Here's Mary, mother of Jesus and his closest female influence in a time of men. But who better than she knows the truth about her son? Interestingly, it is she, a woman, who gave birth to what happens here today. Just a woman, just a mother who changed the history of humanity.

MARY, MOTHER OF JESUS (enters slowly, with the support of Mary Magdalene, to center front): Here, this is fine. I want to be close. They'll be bringing him here, I'm sure.

NARRATOR: Her friend is Mary Magdalene, a woman who has experienced the miraculous work of Christ firsthand. Her Christ has shown her love, and she now holds this gift as her most precious possession.

MARY MAGDALENE: He'll be alright. I know the power of his love. I know what his love—

CAIAPHAS: Kill him! You heard me! Kill the man! Kill him before he kills you! (JESUS enters from back to front center stage followed by GUARD. CAIAPHAS pauses while JESUS crosses in front of him and takes position facing audience, standing, with GUARD standing behind.) Do you people really trust this man? Look what he's done. He's brainwashed our children. You parents no longer understand your own sons and daughters. He's walked all over our traditions, our values, and beliefs. He's given our food and shelter to common derelicts and told us to give them more. Our priests are beginning to sound like him. Our leaders can no longer control the people. He's stolen our sense of survival and thrown it away. And left us with what? A mumbo-jumbo religion of give-unto-others-what-is-rightfully-ours. He talks big about a heaven but he comes from hell. He is the son of the devil!

Listen! This is Passover. How appropriate! The day our God, Jehovah, came to kill the firstborn sons of our Egyptian captors. God kills anyone who wants to enslave us, God's people! It's right we kill this man, this one who threatens our freedom with new teachings, new tricks, new heresies! He's the firstborn son of the devil! Kill him! (Begins to sit.)

MARY MAGDALENE: The Messiah!

CAIAPHAS: Kill him!

MARY MOTHER OF JESUS: No!

JUDAS: No, no, Mary. Now let it be. Let them take him. It'll be better this way, don't you see? They'll try to kill him. They'll take him out and nail him down, but then, just as they try to set him up to die, he'll just step down off of the cross and show them all he's God. They'll have to love him then. Even Caiaphas will have to believe. Let them try to kill him. He'll show them. We'll show them who's God.

CAIAPHAS: There, listen to the man. That'll settle it. If he's the Messiah, like you say he is, if he's the Son of God, I say he has to prove it! Let's put him to the test. God won't let the Messiah die. Crucify him! Make him show us who he is. Show us a miracle, you! You promised miracles. Well, show us one. *(Sits.)*

(GUARD begins binding Jesus.)

PETER: Wait! I mean, ah, wait a minute. Okay? Miracles are one thing, but this man—ah—what's his name?—ah—Jesus, he might not be so bad even without the miracles. Right? I mean, do we really know? Shouldn't we ask him some questions? Like where's he from? Who is he? What's he do for a living? Maybe he's causing a few problems here, but he may be just a normal guy doing a lot of good stuff, too. We ought to check, shouldn't we?

PILATE *(stepping on stage):* Who are you, mister?

PETER: Peter, sir. My name's, ah, Peter. And I, well, some of the things he was saying were, well, making a little sense. I mean, I don't know if miracles are so important. After all, he's said a lot, too. Good things. Things that have helped me understand who and what I am. I mean, well, I don't know if I believe him or anything, but—

PILATE: Yes?

PETER: Well, ah—nothing.

PILATE: You've heard him say he's the Christ?

PETER: The Christ, sir?

PILATE: Did he or didn't he say he was the Messiah?

PETER: I told you I don't know him.

PILATE: Are you one of them, fella?

PETER: No, no, hardly. I'm just trying to keep an open mind. Don't feel anything, really. *(Pause.)* But I can see where this guy's dangerous. Maybe it's best we put him away. Yeah, go ahead. I'm sorry. I guess I spoke out of turn. Don't let me bother you. *(To self and slowly sitting.)* I don't want to bother anyone.

PILATE: Well, that didn't get us anywhere. Anyone else got any suggestions? Seems like I'm about the only innocent one around here. All of you've got some pretty strong opinions about whether this man lives or dies. Well, let's hear some, eh? Give me some proof. What's stopping you? Is the man guilty or not? What's he charged with, anyway? Anyone know? Great. You haul some half-crazed, vagrant up here in front of me and you want to kill him but you've got no reason to. Some civilization you Jews have. Well, you kill him; it's up to you. I've got nothing to do with it. It's not my responsibility. Tell you what, though. You want blood? I'll give you blood. But let's slaughter a real misfit. I'll give you the choice between this character and that slime Barabbas. What do you say? Which do you want back in society?

JUDAS, CAIAPHAS, CROWD *(Mime stands with placard, ''Barabbas.'' Encourages crowd):* Barabbas! Give us Barabbas!

PILATE: You're kidding me. Well, it's up to you. Like I said, I've got nothing to do with it. *(Sits.)*

MARY, MOTHER OF JESUS: No, no, my son! He's my son! *(Rushes forward and falls at feet of Jesus.)*

CAIAPHAS *(jumping back up):* Don't listen to her! Don't you see? She's just trying to protect her son. But we've got to protect ourselves. The man is dangerous. Kill him!

MARY, MOTHER OF JESUS: Jesus!

CROWD: *(MIME with placard, ''Kill him'', stands and*

encourages crowd again. BARABBAS leads chanting.) Kill him! Kill him! *(MARY, MOTHER OF JESUS, reaches up to undo bonds but is slapped away by GUARD.)*

MARY MAGDALENE *(follows MARY, MOTHER OF JESUS, then turns, and cries out.):* Pilate! *(PILATE stands slowly.)* Save him! Pilate, you're one of us. You've got to let him live!

PILATE: I'm no Jew.

MARY MAGDALENE: Help us, Pilate. We're all the same. We're all dying. He's our only hope. What harm can he do?

PILATE: Leave me out of this.

MARY MAGDALENE: It's too late. You're in it already. You're no better than we are.

PILATE: Look, lady, I don't care what you believe. All this sounds to me like a religion for old ladies and cowards. I've got to deal with reality on my own terms, not with any make-believe hocus-pocus belief in the supernatural. I say the man dies. Make of it as you will. I've said enough. *(Starts to exit.)*

MARY MAGDALENE: Save him! Let him go!

PILATE *(impatiently):* Don't you ever know when it's over? It's time to go home, lady. It's finished. Your man is a dead man. *(Exits.)*

JUDAS: That's enough, Mary Magdalene! You've said enough. Let the man carry out his duties. We all have our parts to play. Let him play his.

MARY, MOTHER OF JESUS: Judas! He's the Son of God! More than just my son. The Son of God! Can't you help release him?

JUDAS: It's too late. It's best this way.

MARY, MOTHER OF JESUS: It can't be best this way.

JUDAS: It's too late, I said.

MARY, MOTHER OF JESUS: Judas, who are you? Are you going to murder my son? *(JUDAS exits.)*

(CAIAPHAS stands and faces JESUS. Lets out a loud, crackling laugh and follows with a long, sweeping mocking bow. Exits. The GUARD jerks JESUS towards the door and they exit.)

(PETER rises slowly and walks to the center of the sanctuary and crosses in front of the two weeping MARYS. Pauses. Looks back at the two MARYS. Returns and with MARY MAGDALENE helps MARY, MOTHER OF JESUS out. Exit slowly.)

NARRATOR: It happened two thousand years ago. Kind of a silly story in a way. The story of humanity, really. The story of a few men and women fighting in desperation to understand what has happened to themselves, to their lives, to history. *(MIME slowly comes to life on corner of stage, crosses to front center, and mounts stage. Raises arms and hands above head, completing entire motion smoothly, slowly, and timed to finish with last words of NARRATOR.)*

And now we find ourselves in the crowd. Today, two thousand years later, we find ourselves as a few mortal beings trying to grasp the meaning of a simple rabbi's life, a rabbi who gave us more than words, a rabbi who gave us life.

(Freeze. MIME slowly drops hands. Exits through back.) □

"Don't Sleep Through It All"

• by C. Roland Marcus

(This playlet was prepared for an Easter sunrise service. Held in an outdoor setting, the worshipers were asked to gather in an oval, and the entire worship experience took place that way. The playlet interrupted a fairly standard worship format and was not announced, as such, in the order of service. The cast was garbed in simple tunic costumes and made their entrances by merely stepping between the oval of worshipers.)

(CROSS BEARER brings cross to the center of the circle. Stands it upright. Looks at it carefully.)

TRAVELER: What are you doing?

CROSS BEARER: I'm remembering.

TRAVELER: That's different?

CROSS BEARER: No, not different—just human.

TRAVELER: Anyone can remember. These people came here to celebrate, rejoice, enjoy the coming spring. Not to remember. Could you take your memory some place else? You're interrupting our service.

CROSS BEARER: But memory is the only thing I have left. Would you deny me that?

TRAVELER: Of course not. I only suggested . . . well, can't you see the problem? This is an Easter crowd with trumpets, and lilies, and hosannas . . . that kind of thing.

CROSS BEARER: Do they object to my memories? Let's take a poll. You start over there and ask them. I'll talk to them on this side. If I'm bothering them, then I'll leave.

TRAVELER: That's silly. What are you remembering that's more important than their singing?

CROSS BEARER: Sleepers. Gamblers. Grave watchers.

TRAVELER: That's all?

CROSS BEARER: If you insist. It's your service, I guess.

TRAVELER: That's not the point. We got up early, feeling good, ready for spring. And you come dragging your cross and your gloomy memories through our satisfactions. Don't you have any memories with which we can identify?

CROSS BEARER *(pausing to think):* Well, I suppose . . . wars—hot and cold, long and short. Protests. Assassinations.

TRAVELER *(growing impatient):* Those won't do. Not here, not now. These folk didn't come for all those mournful memories. I think you had better

---

The author is the Pastor of the Dorothy Lane American Baptist Church, Kettering, Ohio.

---

leave and let us get on with the service.

CROSS BEARER: All right. But don't expect much.

TRAVELER: Oh, we've Eastered before, either here or elsewhere. Nothing to it when you know the tune.

CROSS BEARER: And how the script ends, right?

TRAVELER: What script? This is a service—not a melodrama.

CROSS BEARER: Of course, and I'm a nuisance—not a worshiper.

TRAVELER: From what you've said so far, I'd call a person who lives in the past some kind of history freak.

CROSS BEARER: Let me ask you something. Did you get up this morning, put on your Easter costume, and gather here just to watch the sun rise and hear the trumpets play?

TRAVELER *(slowly):* No, it was more than that. I believe it's real.

CROSS BEARER: What's real?

TRAVELER: You know . . . the . . . ah . . . well, you know.

CROSS BEARER: I don't know. That's why I asked.

TRAVELER: Well, it's what Easter means to me.

CROSS BEARER: Oh, that's a striking title.

TRAVELER: Well, everyone knows what Easter means. Christ lived. Christ died. Christ rose again. Didn't you hear the songs?

CROSS BEARER: I heard. I wonder if they did. *(Points vaguely to the distance.)*

TRAVELER: Who?

CROSS BEARER: The sleepers. The gamblers. The grave watchers.

TRAVELER: They're here?

CROSS BEARER: Always.

TRAVELER: Why?

CROSS BEARER: Reminders, I suppose. I'm not really sure.

TRAVELER: Reminders of what?

CROSS BEARER: Why don't you ask them?

(CROSS BEARER remains in place at the center of the circle. TRAVELER moves around the circle, looking for the "sleepers." They appear from behind the circle. They are PETER and JAMES.)

TRAVELER *(looking curiously at PETER):* You must be a sleeper. Right?

PETER: Who told you that?

TRAVELER *(quickly):* No one! It was only a guess. We seem to be having a little trouble with our service. It's been interrupted, which is unfortunate on Easter.

JAMES: Well, we can't help you. *(Curiously.)* Why did you call us sleepers?

TRAVELER (*pointing to CROSS BEARER whose back is turned*): He happened to mention it. But he must be wrong. He's the problem.

PETER: You're sure he's not the answer?

TRAVELER: I'm not sure of anything.

JAMES: I challenge that! You're sure of many things. *There's more faith here than there was back then.* There's nothing uncertain about the cross that fellow's carrying. No doubt you wear a golden one around your neck. It's loaded with faith, hope, and charity.

TRAVELER: That bothers you?

PETER: No, but your attitude does, a little. We know what you were thinking when you called us sleepers. You think we left the Master to face his agonies alone. If the truth were known, you'd as soon call me a coward as a sleeper.

TRAVELER: No, I . . . well . . . he brought the whole thing . . . Can't we just worship and go have our breakfast?

PETER: Sure. Go ahead. Don't let us hold you up.

TRAVELER: Good. Would you like to join us for songs and prayer?

PETER: No. Thank you.

TRAVELER: Why not?

PETER: We don't quite fit here.

TRAVELER: We'll find a place for you in the circle.

JAMES: That's not what we mean. You see, we're just bumblers from the Bible, warts and all. We slept when we should have been "watching." We kept quiet when we should have been speaking, and speaking when we should have been quiet. Everyone here knows us too well. So we don't qualify.

(*Across the circle, the gamblers, dressed the same as Peter, break into the circle. One carries a set of dice with is thrown around casually, the other has a robelike garment thrown over the shoulder.*)

GAMBLER I: You're right, pious person. You *don't* qualify. We saw you that Friday, sniffling like a frightened animal while Jesus died.

GAMBLER II: You and the rest of the crowd wanted to lead the parade to Paradise.

(*PETER hangs his head.*)

GAMBLER I: We heard about you and your conniving buddies, hatching up schemes to be greatest in the kingdom. Your problem was you couldn't stand the risk, and that's what life is all about—risk.

JAMES (*crossing from behind PETER to confront the GAMBLER*): What do you know about risk? Did you leave your livelihood and your family to follow the Master? What risk is there in raffling off a victim's robe? Cheap entertainment. No chance to that at all.

GAMBLER I: Admit it, though. You missed the message. When Jesus spoke of death, you thought he meant the death of your people's slavery—not of death itself.

GAMBLER II: Jesus came to serve, while you fellows were signing up to master the world.

GAMBLER I: Half your crowd turned in their badges and ran for cover at the first sight of blood.

GAMBLER II: And don't forget the one who'd sold the blood before it was ever shed. Where did Judas get to, anyway? (*Looking around the crowd.*) Is there a Judas in the crowd? Judas is more our type. Come on out, Judas. (*Shaking dice.*) I'll roll you double or nothing for those coins you're carrying. How about it, Judas? A little wager to start your heart of a spring morning?

(*One of the grave watchers appears from behind the circle. The gamblers and the grave watchers look each other over carefully. Finally, the GAMBLER speaks.*)

GAMBLER I: That's not Judas.

GAMBLER II: Looks a little like Judas, though.

GAMBLER I: No, the eyes are different. Judas's eyes look always for an angle, a quick way to make a shekel.

GAMBLER II: You're right; those eyes are weak from watching for a world that never was. Come on, we're wasting our time here. Let's go find Judas and get a game going.

WATCHER I: You won't find Judas here, or any place that matters. Oh, Judas's heirs are left from one end of the globe to another, but Judas is not here. I've been watching for . . .

GAMBLER I: For what?

WATCHER I: For cheats . . . quacks . . . fakers.

GAMBLER II: No lack of them. Is that all?

WATCHER I: Well, I've been waiting for hope to happen, but that's a private project.

GAMBLER I: You're wasting your time. Now warding off fakers who steal Saviors from graveyards—that's a worthwhile undertaking. But forget the hope business. The only hope worth talking about is in the hands of luck, with a little help from the human mind.

WATCHER I: I suspect you're right. I keep watching. The pay's not much, but the work is steady.

(*Another watcher appears. No one recognizes her.*)

WATCHER II: The watching is over. Your risks have been satisfied. Don't sleep through it this time.

GAMBLER I: What's she talking about? (*All shrug their shoulders.*) What are you babbling about, woman?

WATCHER I: Move on, lady. We're practical people, with down-to-earth problems.

WATCHER II: Could I speak with you privately for a moment?

PETER: Who?

WATCHER II: All of you.

(*Slowly they nod their willingness to listen. They gather in a circle around the cross. She whispers to them, one at a time, then they step back.*)

GAMBLER I: I don't believe it.

GAMBLER II: Ridiculous!

WATCHER I: Absurd!

TRAVELER: Obviously they doubt your word. Why don't you try these others?

WATCHER II (*Goes to one end of circle and quietly says*): "Christ is risen! Christ is risen, indeed!"

(*This is passed around the circle of worshipers. Individually, each is asked to pass the word to the next person until it has spread around the entire circle.*) □

The Sneakers Tree

Communicating the Meaning of Easter

● by Harry Farra

NARRATOR: This is Easter—the time of the trial, torture, crucifixion, and entombment of Jesus. Then his resurrection. One of the problems of the church has always been how to explain all of that in language that contemporary people can grasp. How to energize the truth—that's our task. The following scene between a professor of English and one of her students shows us that dilemma. Our scene takes place in a college classroom just after the teacher has gone public with her faith. One student remains behind after class has ended.

JOE: Thanks, Mrs. Thompson, for sharing that religious

Harry Farra is Chairman of the Department of Speech Communication, Geneva College, Beaver Falls, Pennsylvania.

stuff with us. I think my parents used to be religious like that.

MRS. T: They aren't anymore?

JOE: No. Dad's tied up with his business, and Mom's an accountant for the bank.

MRS. T: Well, what about you?

JOE: Me?

MRS. T: Yes, you. You're responsible for your own decisions.

JOE: Oh, it's all too confusing for me. Protestants say they have the truth. Moslems say they worship the true God. Catholics say their church was begun by Peter. And they all teach conflicting doctrine. It's complicated stuff like predestination and purgatory, scapegoats, baptism, and three gods who really are only one god. That kind of business, and then there's the Moonies and the Krishnas. I figure either they're all wrong or they're all right. Either way I'll luck out.

MRS. T: Well, let's forget some of that and get to the real issue. If you could sum up what the Protestant churches preach, how would you describe it?

JOE: I don't really understand it. It's got something to do with Jesus dying but not really dying. It all seems weird to me—people sitting around being glad that Jesus died.

MRS. T: I think you've missed the main point. It's not *that* he died, but *why* he died.

JOE: Well, those crazy preachers on TV keep shouting that he died to take away sin. But how does he take it away and where does he take it to? And why? Church people still sin, don't they? How come Jesus didn't take away that sin? Besides, I don't believe in having to get rid of sin. Sins are just a natural part of life. Sin has always been here and always will be. I haven't met a perfect person yet. Then this stuff really gets intellectually spooky when they start talking about Jesus getting up out of his grave and haunting people and then floating up to heaven.

MRS. T: I think we need to take a different angle on our discussion. Tell me, Joe, you're in a fraternity, right?

JOE: Sure, Gamma Delta.

MRS. T: What's your job assignment in the fraternity?

JOE: I'm the Keeper of the Sneakers Tree. I guard it to make sure no one takes the sneakers.

MRS. T: Tell me about the Sneakers Tree.

JOE: Well, at the end of our frat house there is a tree. We have this tradition, see, that when our seniors are about to graduate and go out into the world, they tie their old sneakers together and toss them on the Sneakers Tree.

MRS. T: Why?

JOE: Well, I guess it's symbolic of them leaving one life and going on to another. I guess they imagine that those old beat-up sneakers represent their past college life that they're now done with and that they're going out into their careers and will need to wear different shoes.

MRS. T: So that tree, in a way, has taken upon itself the old lives of these graduating seniors and offers them the hope of a whole new life.

JOE: Sure.

MRS. T: Joe, don't you see? You've just preached the story of Easter to me.

JOE: I have?

MRS. T: Think about it, Joe. The cross is a kind of sneakers tree where people tie up their sins, problems, and burdens and symbolically toss them on God's Sneakers Tree. Those people have left behind their past "old life" and are now graduating to a "new life" in Christ with a "new pair of shoes."

JOE: That sure is funny. I never thought of Jesus' cross and resurrection being just like our Sneakers Tree.

MRS. T: Now that you've thought about it, what are you going to do about it?

For Discussion:

1. What has been your experience in going public with your faith?

2. Mrs. Thompson found the "sneakers tree" to be a good metaphor for talking about the meaning of the cross. Can you find other metaphors relevant to other people? For example, to a lifeguard? a banker? a physician? a steelworker?

3. How clear is the church in communicating the essence of Easter to the nonchurched?

4. Why do nonchurch people often look upon television preachers as crazy? Do these preachers have a communication problem?

5. When it comes to the ultimate end of man in the final judgment, do most non-Christian people think they'll "luck out"?

6. Do church people still sin? If so, then what has the gospel done for them?

7. Is Christianity "intellectually spooky," as Joe insisted?

8. Is it important to nudge people, as did Mrs. Thompson, from thinking about the cross and Easter to doing something about it? □

LET'S DO GODSPELL!

● **by Marcia Patton**

Occasionally spectacular events happen that were never intentionally planned. For the youth group of the First Baptist Church, Salt Lake City, Utah, doing *Godspell* was like that. We weren't thinking of doing a "Lenten program." We were just noodling on different ideas. I said, "How would you like to do a youth cantata?" That was the question that started it all. A group of youths were meeting with me to discuss ideas for expanding our program.

The youth were not sure what a cantata was, and so I tried to explain. Somehow the explanation brought the comment, "Could *Godspell* be called a cantata?" My reply of "not exactly" was not heard in the clamor of "Could we do *Godspell?*" "Let's do *Godspell!*" "We can do it!"

The amazing thing was that somehow that first year,

To secure the rights for producing the play, write to: Charles Hansen, Educational Sheet Music and Books, 1860 Broadway, New York, NY 10023.

even with a student director and the leads going out of town the week before the performance, they did it!

The next year the group went to see the local university production of *Godspell* that was presented near Christmastime. During the intermission Mark said, ''Let's do it again!'' And the others took up the idea. I reminded them of all the work it would take, the hours of practice, all the time they would have to give to it, but they were certain—adamant in fact. So, we set out. Between Christmas and Palm Sunday, practices were held, costumes made, props bought, practices and practices and practices scheduled, sponsors were sought, rights were secured, changes were made, lighting was worked on, and the play was talked about and publicized. On Palm Sunday evening they performed it. They did a splendid job. It was better than the first time around because they knew what they were getting into.

Hurdles

Preparing for a production is easier the second time around. Any production (a simple cantata or something on a grander scale), even the second time around, needs careful attention to the details. One of our first hurdles was securing the rights for the play. We had problems finding the correct address to secure rights. Once the address was secured, we wrote to tell of our intentions and made our contract with the copyright owner. The first time was our greatest expense. After we purchased the music and adapted the script to our use, it was less of a financial hurdle.

We paid for our expenses by selling sponsorships and listing them in the program. There were enough people in the congregation to contribute five dollars each so that we had no trouble meeting our expenses. Their gifts made it possible for us to offer free seating at the performance.

A detail somewhat unique to *Godspell* was magic props. We happened to have a good magic store nearby and managed all right. We had to keep our props in good working order and available. We found a big box the best answer.

Another issue was scenery. The group felt the trustees would be upset if we put holes in the floor for posts for a chain-link fence, and so we compromised by using the stage walls as they were. We found it difficult to get sawhorses sturdy enough for how we had to use them. Again we adapted, this time to a different concept all together. We used plank boards and eight-foot stepladders. We did a lot of fun adaptations in the play and felt much more secure all the way around.

Costumes were made mostly from rags and this and that. We made a few special things but felt best about garments we ''stumbled across.''

The biggest headache of a production like this was the practice schedule. With the calendars and activities of seventh to twelfth graders, at times it seemed easier to give up than to find times that would mesh with ten actors, two musicians, a lighting technician, and three separate school districts. Usually there was some time

on Saturday when the majority of people could be present for most of the time. Many a Saturday morning, afternoon, or evening was taken up with rehearsals. Sometimes we would be together for six or more hours at a time—sharing meals and adjusting the script according to who could be present.

A Part of the Youth Program

We continued with regular fellowship meetings and committed ourselves to not practicing during that time because it would exclude some youth not involved in the play. The group did not want to be exclusive and would gladly find jobs, even adjust the script, for anyone who wanted to help or participate. The script was adapted according to the numbers of males and females we had to do the acting. Our only requirement for participants was to be at as many rehearsals as possible and to have a spirit of cooperation in working together.

The group played as hard (sometimes even harder) on breaks as they worked during rehearsals. The group was creative in adapting parts and in making up games to play on breaks. Our lighting technician was very supportive, somewhat more committed to being at rehearsals than others in the group. We often began or ended rehearsals with prayer.

Benefits

The results of the many hours of practice and arranging was a simple yet beautiful presentation to the congregation and community in our social hall on Palm Sunday evening.

There were a lot of other results as well. One was the whole spirit of working together to get the job done. The support that the acting staff gave each other and the musicians, the support that the musicians gave the actors, and the quiet, ever-present input of the lighting technician made the work of rehearsals and the nervousness of the performance bearable. Although there were many patience-trying times, there were many other times when the members of the group demonstrated their care for each other and their willingness to share with others.

Another benefit was all the Scripture that was memorized. Most of the dialogue of *Godspell* comes word for word from the *New English Bible*. These youth who would not think of memorizing Scripture in their church school classrooms were putting whole parables and discourses to memory because of the ''fun of it all.'' One of the *Godspell* songs is from the Psalms; others can be found with different music in some of our hymnals. These lessons of the Gospels were told and retold in rehearsals.

The group formed into the First Baptist DRAMA club, performed some other plays, and kept coming back to do *Godspell* again—for the local rescue mission, the air force chapel, and local churches.

This Lenten event was a vehicle for youth to be active. Its benefits are being felt in their lives to this day. Even though at first the obstacles seemed overwhelming, it was well worth all the effort to give it a try.   □

"…. Do this in remembrance of me."

Luke 22:19

"Give Us This Day..."

● by Edward David Willis

Whatever else we modern Christians may forget about our heritage, we know the Lord's Prayer by heart. That means a lot. In a Bible the heart stands for the whole person; so knowing this prayer by heart means far more than just having it memorized. It means the prayer's cadences and content are so much a part of us that it quite naturally and spontaneously has become the most basic prayer of the Christian community. Even when we despair of being able to pray as we ought, the Lord's Prayer has a way of surfacing in the crises and triumphs of our lives.

The very familiarity of this prayer, however, sometimes obscures the startling claims it makes and our extraordinary audacity of repeating it in the modern world. To understand what it means to pray it wittingly and honestly, we need to recall that it comes to us in a slightly different and briefer form in Luke than the form most frequently used from Matthew.

In Luke 11 the disciples observe Jesus praying. They ask him to teach them to pray as John the Baptist teaches his disciples to pray. Jesus responds simply: "When you pray, say: 'Father, hallowed be thy name. Thy kingdom come. Give us each day our daily bread; and forgive us our sins, for we ourselves forgive everyone who is indebted to us; and lead us not into temptation' " (Luke 11:2-4). Luke follows the prayer with encouragement about the utter reliability of God's hearing our prayers: Jesus gave examples of how even humans finally will displace themselves to respond to the "importunity" and nagging of others. If even earthly fathers who are evil (verse 13) know how to give good things to their children, how much more so can our heavenly Father be counted on to hear and respond. There is a categorical assurance to Christ's words: "I tell you, Ask and it will be given you; seek, and you will find . . ." (verses 9-10).

Professor David Willis teaches systematic theology at Princeton Theological Seminary.

Reprinted from *A.D.,* © September, 1980. Used by permission.

Luke has a Gentile audience in mind, and he records portions of Christ's teaching that assure men and women of all nations that they can call on the God revealed by the Jewish Messiah. Matthew writes with a different agenda. His main purpose is to show how Jesus fulfills prophecies made to Israel in such a way that true righteousness is set in motion as opposed to the false interpretation of the Law. That intent shapes the context in which Matthew presents the Lord's Prayer.

In chapter 6, Matthew deals with the nature of true piety: "Beware of practicing your piety before men in order to be seen by them; for then you will have no reward from your Father who is in heaven" (Matthew 6:1). This applies to almsgiving, to praying, and to fasting. He urges secret prayer: "But when you pray, go into your room and shut the door and . . . do not heap up empty phrases as the Gentiles do; for they think that they will be heard for their many words. . . . your Father knows what you need before you ask him. Pray then like this . . ." (Matthew 6:6-15).

What is most important about both forms of the Lord's Prayer is the new relationship with God through Christ to which it attests. Christ has called these people and equipped them to share in his own ministry. Their personal life stories have been caught up in his story, so that they have been given new identities. That is the fundamental fact which is presupposed both in the disciples' use of this prayer and in our repetition of it.

The extent and quality of this new relationship is summarized in the form of address which Christ instructs his followers to use: "Father," in the intimate form "Abba." This God is the Holy One of Israel, the Lord of Hosts, the one whose name is holy, who dwells in the high and holy place. God is the one whose ways are not our ways and whose thoughts are not our thoughts. But in this prayer we are invited and freed to call on this God as "Abba," which almost means "Daddy" or "Papa."

This new relationship is not, of course, a sentimental chumminess with the divine. Nor is it based on an abstract

hope that God ought to be intimate with us apart from the mediation of God's love through Christ. We can call on God as a loving, powerful, caring parent because of Christ's own active obedience to God's will. The One whom the disciples are instructed to address familiarly is the One to whom Christ prays in his own most severe testing, "My Father, if it be possible, let this cup pass from me" (Matthew 26:39).

The disciples are taught by this freely obedient mediator to know and trust God as the one who sees and cares for all things with a loving providence, which is the basis for their not being anxious about the morrow (Matthew 6:25-34).

Above all, God's forgiveness and acceptance can be robustly counted on, for God is like the father who is lavish in his mercy in the so-called parable of the prodigal son (Luke 15:11-32). This theme is expanded in John's Gospel in Christ's prayer for the disciples (John 17).

In Paul's writings the concept of "adoption," of our being received into God's household as sons and daugh-

ters, is a central description of reconciliation. Paul's experience is ours—often as not we do not know how to pray. Our confusion, fatigue, and rebellion do not break the new relationship, however, for Christ and the Spirit intercede on our behalf and cry "Abba!" (Romans 8:15).

This fact, the priority of God's acceptance and favor, is absolutely fundamental to all Christian prayer. We are heard by God not because we come up with "worthy" prayers. Our prayers are worthy because we offer them in the name of the mediator, who enables us to come boldly to the throne of grace and repeat after him, "Our Father. . . ."

The Intimate God

Addressing God as Father has become a scandal for many in the church today. Many negative connotations are engendered by masculine language. It is quite possible, for example, for male language about God to carry so much descriptive freight about one who is judge,

scholarship which points out that both the Old and New Testaments use female as well as male imagery for God. She finds it a healing experience to call on God as Mother. "I am aware," Swidler writes, "that the word Mother refers to nothing new: Simply that God as my creator and shaper, that which supports me always, source of wisdom and grace. Yet, when I consider how she lives in me and I in her, how the world is hers, and how her image is seen in all of us, I find myself healing, becoming whole once again. I learn nothing new, yet all is renewed."

Living Day By Day

Many Christians today will not find Ms. Swidler's experience their own, but it is important that God be acknowledged and relied upon as one with the personal qualities which she mentions and which are entirely consistent with the relationship designated by the familiar and intimate address to which Christ invites his disciples: "Abba."

I have concentrated on the relationship which is presupposed in the opening words of the Lord's Prayer. The specific petitions that follow are detailed ways by which that relationship bears fruit in everyday life: God's name is hallowed among us. God's will is done on earth as in heaven. It is because of this established relationship that we simply ask for daily bread, the wherewithal for living day by day; for forgiveness within a context in which we also practice the healing ministry of forgiveness; for not being put beyond our strength to the severe testings of external persecution and internal betrayal; and for liberation from oppressive structures and from the ingeniously subtle enchantments that would cause us to refuse our new identity in Christ, turning our backs on the social and personal demands of the gospel. The wondrous thing is that our very human petitions are actually given weight and subordinate power in God's own unfolding purposes for all creation.

We of course receive comfort from a renewal of the covenant in this prayer. But more than that, God actually chooses to work through the prayers of the faithful community, and they become useful to God—as our other works are—so long as they arise out of the context of faith.

The final ascription of praise is a confession of the faith with which the Lord's Prayer begins. It closes the bracket, as it were, of the equation within which our particular petitions are given weight. It reasserts that it is to God that all honor and power and glory belong.

The "Amen" is a hearty cry that the preceding act of trust is firmly based on the assurance that God has indeed heard us when we pray this prayer. Luther's observations on the "Amen" are to the point. In a little tract written for his barber, Luther says, "You must always make the *Amen* strong, never doubting that God is surely listening to you with all grace and saying "yes" to your prayer. Remember that you are not kneeling or standing there alone, but that all Christendom, all devout Christians are standing there with you and you with them in one unanimous united prayer which God cannot ignore. That is what 'Amen' means."

arbitrary controller, and aggressive ruler that it precludes the very intimacy which Jesus intended the familiar form "Abba" to convey. We surely have not finished the task of filtering out and reinterpreting much of the unnecessarily masculine language in which so much of the Judeo-Christian tradition has come to us.

At least it is clear that calling God "Abba" is not a declaration of God's gender. That word speaks of the quality of God's relationship to us as a loving, caring, provident, correcting and nurturing person. For some this may mean freedom to experience and to call on God in terms which they most immediately associate with the feminine. Arlene Swidler's brief chapter entitled "Praying to God, My Mother" in *How Do I Pray?* will prove useful for many women and men.

Ms. Swidler remains a practicing Roman Catholic despite her deep disappointment over her church's reluctance to make radical changes in ecclesiastical authority and in the male language which still dominates the Mass. She takes heart from some recent biblical

A CELEBRATION
of
PENTECOST

● by Margaret Fox

"What is Pentecost?" the teacher asked. "The building that the army works in," came the answer. So we discovered that in our congregation very few people, children or adults, really knew what Pentecost is.

How could we change this? We could have a celebration that would involve the entire congregation in preparation and would be something to look forward to. It would take people beyond Easter into another of the

Margaret Fox is Director of Christian Education, First Presbyterian Church, Wheaton, Illinois.

Reprinted from *Alert,* February, 1981.

church's seasons. Our church has both a membership of people who are mobile, coming from a variety of denominational backgrounds and traditions, and a group who have been members for years. So Pentecost Sunday became a focal point for the church, an occasion in which everyone could share.

Brainstorming

Persons from various groups—the Women's Association, choirs, church school, youth groups, couples, and the men's organizations—were gathered for a brainstorming session. What might we do to provide an experience of the meaning of Pentecost for our congregation? The brainstorming began with a study of the account in Acts 2 of the gift of the Holy Spirit to the disciples. What happened on that first occasion? After searching the Scriptures for the first-century experience, we tried to discover what it means to us nineteen hundred years later.

Ideas and suggestions came first, and after three Saturday morning meetings the purposes, the plan of action, and the responsibilities were worked out and assignments of responsibility made. There would be a procession of banners made by families and individuals in the congregation, a celebration of Communion using Scottish shortbread as one of the elements, and a young people's brass band. In order to help people create banners, there would be a series of workshops.

A Variety of Banners Produced in Workshops

At the workshops on banner making, illustrations were provided of a wide variety of symbols and their meanings. There were several people skilled in graphics to help people with design. Our graphics people were to aid the "unartistic" over the first hurdle. A tribute to their skill was that no two banners were of the same design; they did not impose their ideas on people but helped them to develop their own. A family who had recently moved into the community used "Bloom Where You Are Transplanted" as its theme. A woman skilled in needlework designed a description of her pilgrimage of faith from baptism into the Christian life. It was complete with a dove with real feathers, representing the Holy Spirit. A church school class's banner shouted, "Happy Birthday, Church!" The variety was evident.

On the Day of Pentecost

As the day of Pentecost dawned, we were hopeful of good weather, sunshine preferred! We did have contingency plans for rain, but sunshine would be the frosting on the cake, the blessing on our procession.

Banners that families and individuals had made to be carried in the procession had been arriving during the week. Their theme was "What the Christian Faith Means to Me."

The publicity team had done a good job. Articles in the local newspaper had invited the community to our church to share the celebration and to see the three banners hanging from the portico of the sanctuary. The seven-branched candlestick, the descending dove, and the seven tongues of fire, all symbols of the Pentecost experience, were depicted on the colorful banners. As the congregation arrived, the banners would remind them that this would be a different service of worship. An artist in the church had designed these banners, her first attempt at religious art. One of the women's groups had assembled them, and two families had hung them.

On that Pentecost Sunday our junior highs arrived early. They had been designated as "gofers," and they were a vital part of the day, keeping things together and moving. They began inflating balloons with helium and organizing the banners so the children of the church school could carry them easily.

The service of worship began with the entrance of the elements for Communion. We were all reminded of our heritage as the Scottish shortbread was presented as part of the Eucharist. New members were received into the fellowship of the church, a very appropriate act for Pentecost, and the sermon was based on Acts 2:1-4.

Near the end of the service, the children of the church school followed the pastor and led the congregation in a procession around the block. Each child carried either a balloon or a banner, and the youth and adults who wanted them were handed balloons to carry. The choir, senior high and adults, led us in singing "We Are One in the Spirit" as we marched, and the brass band kept us in time. As the procession returned to the patio area for the benediction, the mood was one of celebration and joy. Afterward, as they shared the coffee the deacons provided, people examined one another's banners, discussing what they meant and how they were made.

Did We Do What We Set Out to Do?

Our stated purposes were: (1) to interpret to the congregation, adults and children, the meaning of Pentecost; (2) to provide a means for families to share with one another the meaning of their individual faith; (3) to provide a means for individuals and families to share with other persons in the church and community the meaning of their faith and their experience in the church; (4) to provide an activity whereby the whole church family (both worshiping congregation and church school) could share in a celebration; (5) to demonstrate that "church is fun!"

Through the newsletter, a presentation in an earlier service of worship, discussion in church school classes, and conversation with individuals and various groups, we deepened our understanding of Pentecost and the heritage of celebrating it. The word took on the meaning of the empowering of the church by the gift of the Holy Spirit, a special time of commitment (as many early Christians became members or were baptized at Pentecost), the founding of the church in mission, or the birthday of the church.

On Monday one member called to thank the church for the experience. That day at her office she had gotten into a discussion with her fellow workers and she had been able to explain what had happened at Pentecost and what that event meant to her. She said that it was the first time she had been able to tell others in her work situation something about the Christian faith and what it meant to her.

At workshops for banner making, there had been a period of time spent reading the second chapter of Acts, answering open-ended questions to help focus our thinking and understanding about Pentecost and to develop new insights, and singing some hymns related to the celebration.

As families made their banners in the workshops, it was exciting to see parents and children, brothers and sisters, working together trying to develop a banner that said something of what their faith meant to them. And there were many lively discussions as they sought to choose or create symbols or slogans that carried the meaning they were intending.

The discussion by people in the various groups and

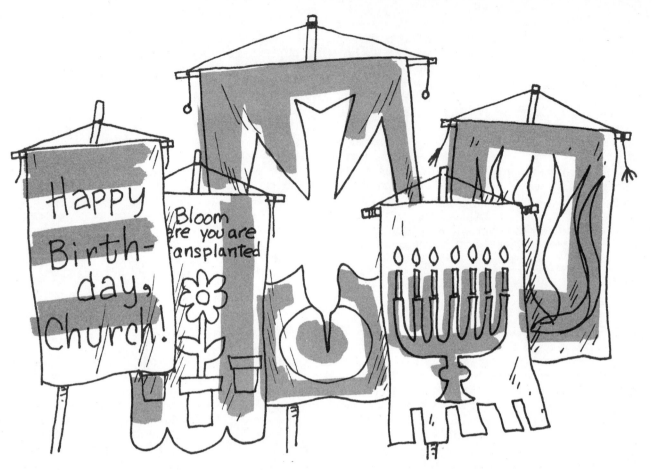

classes, the excitement of telling what the banners meant after the service of worship, and reported conversations with neighbors as members explained that what we were doing provided opportunity for witness—a word that to many people in our congregation had meant being buttonholed by very aggressive Christians on street corners and being asked if one was saved.

Church school meets at the same time as worship and we tend to develop two congregations, one older and one younger, those who worship and those who study. Our celebration of Pentecost was one attempt to bring these two congregations together.

And in a congregation that is Presbyterian and accustomed to doing things "decently and in order," the idea that worship and being in church is fun was enjoyable to develop. We had a real sense of the joy of celebration, of sharing, and of fun.

Our Learnings

We learned many things through our experience. One of these was that by planning far enough ahead we had the opportunity to include and contact all the groups in the church so that people heard about the celebration in a variety of ways and from many different people. This helped to build momentum and a feeling of involvement and anticipation even for those people who were not going to make banners.

Some people in our congregation do not like the service of worship "messed around with." By talking about what we were going to do and the reasons for it and by preparing the ground so people were not surprised but were anticipating the occasion, most people were able to share fully in the event. When the congregation was invited to join in the procession around the block, all joined in. That for some was the high point of the day—participation by everyone.

Other Ways of Celebrating

The Pentecost season may also be a time for an emphasis on new members (especially adult). What a joyful occasion in the spirit of the first Pentecost is the baptism of an adult Christian! A special thrust for evangelism in your local community can be an exciting focus leading to joining the church on Pentecost.

The heritage of a church can be celebrated. One year our celebration entailed more emphasis on the history of the Christian church and our local church. The children sang the chorus of the Avery and Marsh song "The Great Parade" as they carried banners representing various people who have strengthened the church through the years. Each class chose a person for whom class members would create a symbol to be presented on a banner. The persons ranged from Noah to Mary, the mother of Jesus, from John Knox to Mary Brewster Goalding, a person who had served as our church school superintendent for many years. As each class carried its banner, the name was read and a brief statement was made telling why the class chose that particular person.

At Pentecost the church was empowered to move out of the upper room and into the streets with the gospel message and life-style. A celebration of the mission thrust of the local church and the total church may help to bring that same empowerment to us—an empowerment that comes from the Holy Spirit. □

"Speaking in Tongues"
A Pentecost Drama

Characters: A Narrator (Peter), Person 1, Person 2, Andrew.

The four players can be dressed in biblical costumes. The NARRATOR is Peter. He may read from the lectern, or he may be out of sight, reading through a microphone from the rear of the sanctuary.

NARRATOR: You ask about the day of Pentecost. Yes, I was there. Jesus had forgiven me my denial, and the days he spent with us were never to be forgotten. Then he left. But he had told us not to leave Jerusalem, but to wait for God's promise to be fulfilled. Jesus had said that John baptized with water, but we should be baptized with the Holy Spirit and become witnesses of him. When he had said these things, a cloud appeared, and he was gone. Then two men in white apparel suddenly stood near us saying: "You men of Galilee, why stand you gazing into heaven? This same Jesus who is taken from you into heaven will come back, just as you have seen him go."

We had chosen Matthias to fill the vacant spot in the twelve left by Judas. When the day of Pentecost came, we were all together. But wait! Let me show you others who were there! Hear their story!
(Two people enter.)

PERSON 1: I wish you could have been there! I tell you that I have never seen anything like it! I was not inside, but I heard the great noise and—

PERSON 2: *(skeptically):* What kind of noise?

PERSON 1: Like the rushing of mighty winds! I expected a torrent of rain to fall, but nothing happened. I looked inside, and it was like tongues of fire sitting upon those men!

PERSON 2: Are you crazy? Never before has such a tale been told!

PERSON 1: I saw what I saw, and I heard what I heard. They began to speak in foreign languages, those big common fishermen! They couldn't have known other languages! Everyone knows Simon and Andrew, James and John! How could they be speaking so?

PERSON 2: Gibberish, that's what it must have been. Gibberish!

PERSON 1: *(shouting angrily):* It was not gibberish! I myself heard what the crowd said! There were people from Parthia, Mesopotamia, Judea, Asia, Egypt, even Libya. There were some from Rome and Crete and Arabia! Every person heard in his or her native tongue!

PERSON 2: *(laughing cynically):* Next I suppose you will tell me their ears were bewitched!

PERSON 1: Why should they be? They did not believe in this uncouth band of fellows who followed a carpenter who was said to have risen from the dead.

PERSON 2: They were probably all drunk.

PERSON 1: *(shaking head):* No. The multitude said that very thing, but the big fisherman called Peter pointed out it was only the third hour. I heard many say, "How can these simple Galileans speak such pure Greek?" Another one laughed at him. "Greek! That's not Greek. It's the purest of Aramaic!" Another spoke up, saying: "Can't you hear? They must be from Cyrene. They speak the language of my birthplace."

PERSON 2: I think you're mad!

PERSON 1: I will prove it to you! Andrew—
(Andrew enters.)

PERSON 1: Aren't you one of the disciples of the carpenter Jesus? Tell us what happened the other day. This stupid friend of mine does not believe that your people spoke with many tongues.

ANDREW: *(slowly, impressively, with a deep voice):* It is true. It was the Holy Spirit that was promised to us. We spoke as the Spirit directed us. All of the people heard in their own languages. What was given us was for the benefit of all. It was of God. *(Exit.)*

PERSON 1: See, did I not tell you?
(The two pantomine disagreement with gestures. First one argues; second one shakes head, unconvinced.)

NARRATOR: That is the way it happened, but I felt impelled to speak to that multitude and tell them it was the fulfilling of the prophecy of Joel, that in the last days God would pour out the Holy Spirit on all

flesh, that their sons and daughters should prophesy, their young men see visions, and their old men dream dreams. God promised wonders in heaven and signs in the earth below. But whosoever called on the name of Jesus should be saved. I spoke to them of Jesus the Christ, whom God had raised up. Some of them asked, ''What shall we do?'' I told them: ''Repent and be baptized every one of you in the name of Jesus Christ for the remission of sins, and you shall receive the gift of the Holy Spirit.''

PERSON 1: Peter even said to the multitude that the promise was for all of us and for our children, as many as God should call!

PERSON 2 *(shrugging shoulders):* What has that to do with us? I have no desire to be dipped in the water. I don't see how it could change my miserable life or make it better. Why should I care to speak with tongues or have this Holy Spirit in my life? I have lived a good life. What need have I to repent? *(Turns to walk away; then he turns back.)* For that matter, what need have you to repent? What will it gain you? *(Exit.)*

PERSON 1 *(slowly, thoughtfully):* Yet there was something about those people: those who call themselves disciples. I wonder—if I were to speak with other tongues, would I be like them? Even if the only tongue I spoke with were a kinder one, would I be happier, and those around me? Someday, when I have provided for my family, when I have laid up treasures—maybe someday, I will try and find out. *(Exit.)*

NARRATOR *(sighing):* Three thousand souls were baptized that day, but many others turned away, unable to understand. My heart ached for them, those lost sheep Jesus had given to our charge. How can I fail to have compassion? Was I not also weak? Did I not also bitterly weep when the cock crowed? Did I not have to answer three times my Lord's question, ''Do you love me?'' I have often thought he asked me three times because it was three times I had denied him. *(Pause.)*

Yes, we spoke in tongues as the Spirit directed. We were filled with the Spirit, and a mighty wind filled the house. But more important, it filled our hearts. No road we would travel, no dusty lane, or busy street would dishearten us. We had been given a living Presence. No more would we walk alone. The day of Pentecost was to live on through us. Because of it, many would be saved. The prophecy was fulfilled, and I know it was true, for I was there—that day to be remembered. □

Silhouette in Spring

I saw a hill;
  And on the hill
    A lonely tree,
  Encircled by
    The endless sky.
Golgotha.
  Calvary.
    Eternity.

   C. W. Vandenbergh